Life among the

Ancient

Two accounts of
an Anasazi
archaeological
research project

Ones

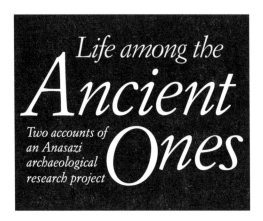

Life among the Ancient Ones

Two accounts of
an Anasazi
archaeological
research project

BY BOB GREENLEE

Any proceeds from the sale of this book will be provided as a gift to the Crow Canyon Archaeological Center in Cortez, Colorado so they may carry on with the important archaeological research projects in which they are engaged.

Cover illustration by Chuck Trout, Visibility Design, Boulder, Colorado

ISBN 0-9647320-0-9 (Hardcover)
ISBN 0-9647320-1-7 (Paperbound)
LCN 95-94592

Published and distributed by
Hardscrabble Press
2076 Hardscrabble Drive
Boulder, Colorado 80303

Printed by Johnson Printing Company, Boulder, Colorado

Manufactured in the United States of America

Dedication

This book is dedicated to Diane
who has learned to share her wisdom and
understanding of so many things.

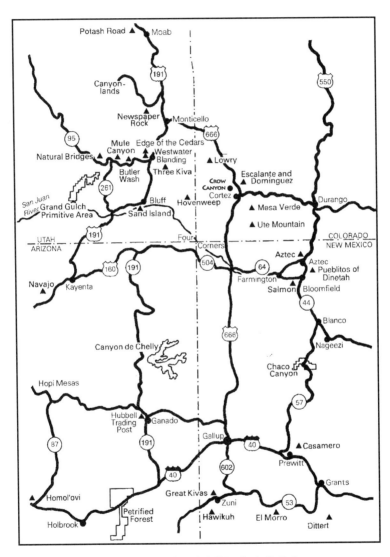

FOUR CORNERS AREA

Nᴏɴᴇ ᴏꜰ ᴛʜᴇ ᴅᴇᴀᴅ *can rise up and answer our questions, but from all that they have left behind, their imperishable or slowly dissolving gear, we may perhaps hear voices which are now only able to whisper when everything else has been silent.*

— Bᴊᴏ̈ʀɴ Kᴜʀᴛᴇɴ, 1984

Iɴ ᴛʜɪꜱ ɪꜱᴏʟᴀᴛᴇᴅ ʟᴀɴᴅ, *the past has been a hoary hermit to the very verge of the newest creations of nature and the latest institutions of man. The flint utensils of the Age of Stone lie upon the surface of the ground. The peoples that made and used them have not yet entirely disappeared.* — Sᴀᴍᴜᴇʟ Hᴀᴠᴇɴ, 1864

introduction

This is largely a work of fiction.

The portions that are not will be obvious, and those that provide an account of life in prehistoric times will be equally obvious.

There is cause for uncertainty, however, because the account of prehistoric life might not be a work of fiction at all. The people and events written about could have occurred just as they are described.

No one will ever know if the people, the crops, the weather, or any of the cosmic forces of nature described here did not happen exactly as they are portrayed.

preface

On this warm and clear July summer night I observe a single gray cloud that moves leisurely across a bright and nearly full moon. The light flickers rhythmically as this thin cloud mass moves south and east toward a National Park we know as Mesa Verde.

When I listen closely, perhaps even a bit more intently than usual, I can hear distant footsteps snapping brittle twigs on the soft and slightly sandy soil of this place. I also hear muted voices that are carried on the gentle breeze which moves through the scrub oak and pinyon pines that help me shape memories of human activity now ending a full and task-filled day.

At this moment, I am very close to sleep in a comfortable place between our Mother Earth and Father Sky. As my mind wanders, I cannot keep from creating images of the past framed by the tangible realities of this place. Not only is the land real, but so are the artifacts of once-inhabited structures and the randomly scattered remains of prior human activity. It is not difficult for me to recall how life might have been lived several thousands of years before by the people who worked and slept on this very soil.

I am here this evening for a variety of rather inconceivable reasons, not all of which I fully understand and thus cannot easily explain. This place is a few miles north and west of the City of Cortez, Colorado in a unique residential subdivision known as Indian Camp Ranch. These 1,185 acres were once crop and grazing lands that were recently subdivided into 31 individual home sites each consisting of about 35 acres. There's nothing particularly remarkable about this, except for the fact that Indian Camp Ranch is no ordinary residential subdivision.

Archie and Mary Hanson are two California real estate developers, entrepreneurs, and promoters who conceived of this particular residential development that combines the usual network of roads, fences, signs, and boundary-markers with 210 documented prehistoric archaeological sites of the Archaic Pueblo Peoples of the southwestern United States. The Navajo Indians—who came to this area much later and are not the descendants of these people—call these former residents the Anasazi which has been roughly translated to mean "the ancient ones." An even more intriguing translation of the Navajo word suggests that the term Anasazi might mean "ancient enemies."

No matter how these prehistoric people might be described by others, they represent one of the most significant and most intriguing Native American populations ever known and who populated the Four Corners area of the southwestern United States for thousands of years.

These ancient people built a number of remarkable communities in the arid lands of the Four Corners region, creating such magnificent places as Chaco Canyon, the cliff dwellings of Mesa Verde, and Canyon de Chelly. About 700 years ago, around the year 1300 A.D., these Anasazi people had almost completely abandoned most of the communities they built and simply moved on. No one is certain exactly why they left, although a combination of factors was most likely responsible. But the people did not disappear entirely, nor did they become extinct. Their descendants continue living in the region to this day and are the Hopi Indians of northeastern Arizona, the Zuni of western New Mexico, and the many Pueblo People of New Mexico.

Most of these prehistoric Anasazi people did not live just in the confines of larger communities such as Chaco Canyon or at Mesa Verde. They also lived in thousands of scattered communal units throughout the Four Corners area that encompasses tens of thousands of square miles of Colorado, Utah, Arizona, and New Mexico. The lots at Indian Camp Ranch represent but a small sample of the many habitation sites that exist throughout this vast region.

As the men, women, and children who participated in the Western expansion throughout the nineteenth century moved to this area, many of these ancient sites were both a nuisance and source of fascination for the farmers and ranchers who ultimately came to live and work on the land. Collecting artifacts of early man, including the Anasazi, was not a difficult task for there were literally tens of thousands of them strewn all across the land. Pottery sherds, arrowheads, and other lithic items, along with wonderfully decorated and intact pottery pieces were easily acquired, studied, and even sold to collectors all over the world.

In the latter part of the nineteenth century, and throughout the twentieth century, these artifacts became even more coveted and gave rise to the deplorable practice of pot hunting and the resulting destruction of important historical sites. No one will ever know the full extent of the devastation that has taken place over the many years of this unregulated exploitation. To a large extent this wanton destruction of our cultural heritage has been halted because we now more fully recognize that the artifacts of our unique cultural history deserve to live forever. As a nation, we've come to recognize the importance of learning from our many ancestors, and a variety of protective measures have been adopted both nationally and locally to preserve our fragile historical past. It is Archie and Mary Hanson's understanding of, and their sensitivity to these matters, that have been a foundation from which the Indian Camp Ranch development was launched.

To the best of anyone's knowledge, Indian Camp Ranch is the first and the only private residential development designed to include archaeological preservation as a primary objective. When you purchase one of the residential lots, as my wife Diane and I did in 1993, you are required to accept the terms and conditions of a number of restrictions and protective covenants that are all designed to ensure that we appropriately coexist with the physical remains of our unique archaeological heritage.

Among the requirements is a condition that all artifacts found on any of the lots must be donated to the Indian Camp Ranch Museum that will eventually be built on the site. Property owners have the ability to keep any of the materials for their own enjoyment but upon the death of the remaining spouse, all artifacts must be returned to the museum for display, or made available for future research. One purpose behind this restriction is to ensure that no artifacts will ever be sold for profit. The Hansons' firm desire is to protect the integrity of their development and see that no commercialization of artifacts might relegate the project to nothing more than managed pot hunting.

If property owners want to excavate any site on their property, and there is no requirement that they do so, they must have the guidance of a professional archaeologist from start to finish. Each property owner is encouraged to fully participate in these exploration activities under the supervision of a professional, and a thorough research report must ultimately be written. In addition, any structures uncovered and exposed must be fully protected from deterioration by constructing a roof or having the structures completely stabilized. No home, garage, driveway, or septic field can be located on an identified site. With these and other appropriate requirements, Indian Camp Ranch is not for everyone, and there are probably a mere handful of unusual people like myself and Diane who would gladly put up with such restrictions and limitations. A common thread naturally exists between the Hansons' development and those people who are likely to become property owners. That link is the Crow Canyon Archaeological Center whose campus is located directly next door to the Indian Camp Ranch.

Crow Canyon is a world-renowned, private, nonprofit archaeological organization whose primary mission is to initiate and conduct significant archaeological research in the southwestern United States and then share the results of those efforts through developing innovative public and professional educational programs. Particularly interesting is the fact that Crow Canyon actively communicates with and involves Native American communities in many of their efforts. In addition, because Crow Canyon is an independent organization, it can initiate partnerships with educational institutions, government bodies, or other organizations that share common interests.

Founded in 1982 to conduct its long-term and large-scale archaeological research in the American Southwest, Crow Canyon has offered a variety of unique and inviting programs to educators, Native Americans, and also the general public. One of the most successful long-term efforts has been their Cultural Exploration programs that are offered to anyone with an interest in Indian history, Southwest archaeology, or just a curiosity about the world they live in. Each year hundreds of adults and youngsters from all over the world participate in actual dig sites close to the campus. Many of the participants return year after year; some with their families who make a unique educational experience out of the various programs.

For many others, who may not want to participate in an archaeological dig, professional archaeologists from several educational institutions assist in conducting one or two-week field seminars throughout the Four Corners area. These educational seminars visit most of the major and more familiar prehistoric sites along with many out-of-the-way locations not generally accessible to the public. During the summer months, educators from around the country are invited to the campus for both laboratory and field work along with discussions about the current status of archaeological endeavors. A particularly appealing part of Crow Canyon's efforts is involved in helping to identify ways in which young people, including Native American kids, can more fully understand and appreciate the need to conduct research into our shared cultural heritage. Crow Canyon's vision is to become a nationally and internationally recognized center for the development of new tools, strategies, and ideas on how to advance understanding of our common human past and enhance our mutual appreciation of all cultures.

I have always had a fascination with the American Southwest.

For many years it was for me a rather foreboding and uninviting place, desert-like, with not much immediate appeal. How people could actually think of living in such places was beyond me. On summer vacations, my family would drive through parts of this lifeless area in the Four Corners and I could hardly wait to rejoin civilization in places like Albuquerque or Santa Fe. It was much later when I became fascinated with the handicrafts of the contemporary Native American people and began to admire the splendid weavings of the Navajo, the intricate wood carvings of the Hopi, the tactile fetish carvings of the Zuni, and of course the magnificent pottery of the modern Pueblo People. That interest translated into wanting to know more about the land, the people, culture, and history of the entire Southwest.

In the spring of 1992, I signed up as a participant in one of the Crow Canyon field seminars. From the very beginning, my interest in the region grew from one of expanding admiration to a sincere desire to know much more about this intriguing land.

Within about a year I was asked to join the Board of Trustees of the Crow Canyon Archaeological Center. I consider my participation to be one of my most rewarding volunteer efforts. It was through this involvement with Crow Canyon that I eventually met Archie and Mary Hanson, which ultimately led to our purchasing a lot at the Indian Camp Ranch.

Our 35-acre parcel contains at least nine Anasazi archaeological sites with habitation dates ranging from the Basketmaker III Period (A.D. 650–725) to the Pueblo II Period (A.D. 900-1150). There are hundreds of prehistoric pottery sherds scattered throughout the property along with lithic materials and a number of surface features that help to confirm the existence of prior human habitation.

One of these sites held great promise for further exploration but it was unfortunately destroyed in 1986. This site consisted of both large and small living areas and storage areas known as a room block. It also showed evidence of a kiva depression and a dense but deeply buried trash-heap called a "midden." The site was located in an undisturbed sagebrush and pinyon-juniper area but it was also known that the site had been vandalized, exposing two of the room blocks and a portion of the trash midden. It seems that in 1986, the prior landowners gave permission to have this site bulldozed by a local pot hunter. True to form, the site was rendered useless for research purposes because a trench was dug, the intact artifacts taken away, and no documentation ever produced or even attempted. Had some of the other known sites in this area been similarly disturbed, they too would probably have been rendered useless for any scientific or research purpose.

Fortunately, the other eight sites had not been disturbed and we commissioned a preliminary investigation of them. We were delighted to be introduced to Woods Canyon

Archaeological Consultants, a professional contract archaeological team. The firm is operated by Jerry Fetterman, and his wife Linda Honeycutt, who live north of the Indian Camp Ranch near Yellow Jacket, Colorado. In the spring of 1994 we contracted with them to conduct field testing which would provide further insight into each of four promising sites of the eight we considered worthy of future exploration.

The primary method of field testing was done with a simple 2 3/4-inch auger that can be hand-drilled several feet into the ground. When the bucket becomes full, it is removed and the sample examined. Any changes in soil composition are recorded for later interpretation. Sometimes, evidence of charcoal, ceramic fragments, bone, or other material is retrieved, providing immediate insight on what lies below. The drilling was done after a north–south and east–west reference line was placed through the area of each site. Auger holes were drilled at 4- or 5-meter intervals. If there were no subsurface materials that might indicate substructures, a parallel line offset from 4 to 8 meters was established and became the focus for additional test drilling.

Final results of these auger tests were reported to us in April. Initial testing of one of the sites—officially identified as Site 5MT3873—looked very promising. The report indicated that below the surface, it was likely that a "multi-component Basketmaker III and Pueblo II habitation site exists" which simply means over a four-hundred-year period of human occupation and activity was likely to be uncovered if a more thorough investigation were made. A total of 98 separate auger holes had been dug which identified a total of four possible subsurface structures and six possible features. This was very exciting news to an amateur archaeologist who could hardly contain his desire to grab trowel and bucket, abandon all current responsibilities, and get to work.

Reason prevailed, and a more realistic schedule of exploration was established. Diane and I would join the Woods Canyon team in mid-July and begin learning the process of digging, documenting, and slowly uncovering one small and rather insignificant part of our prehistoric human history.

CHAPTER *one*

Early summer in the Four Corners area is usually warm and dry. Not much rain will fall until August when the upper-level winds shift and bring much needed moisture from the south. The hottest month of all is usually June when the sky remains nearly cloudless, the humidity nonexistent, and the earth itself gives up what little moisture there is to the light breezes which blow across the land. The smallest tree produces modest but inviting shade that is not only welcoming, but nearly impossible to resist and a brief nap equally impossible to avoid.

On this particular day in mid-June, a young man now in his seventeenth season, and who is called by the name Hosta, glances up at a glaring sun holding his right hand above his head to protect his eyes from the intense light. He is standing at the corner of a field of corn that his uncle, paternal grandfather, and cousins helped to plant over a month before. Earlier this morning, at sunrise, Hosta came out to the field and joined in the task of loosening soil around the tender young plants, building earth up around the shoots while at the same time pulling any weeds whose roots might compete for the precious moisture that is held deep in the sandy soil. The seed itself was planted quite deeply within the earth, almost a foot below the surface where there is usually adequate moisture for germination and solid root formation.

The planting date had been set by one of the many priests of the village where Hosta and his family live. There were a countless number of signs that this "Sun Watcher" priest must observe. The return of certain types of birds from the south is one of the important signs. Observing the growth of certain spring plants is also carefully watched. Clouds and certain cloud formations are noted along with the constantly changing winds that are tested daily. All these factors are keenly observed by these priests who are highly revered by the people of the villages.

Along with setting the all-important date for planting, medicine men perform a variety of ceremonies necessary to prepare the seeds for planting. These ancient rituals, if they are done carefully, act as a form of crop insurance. Most of these rituals we today call fertility rites and their aim is to make sure that the gods of reproduction and fertility have been pleased. If they are not, the seeds may simply rot in the ground so chanting, dancing, and various offerings are made to these gods. The offerings may include corn pollen, prayer sticks, tossing corn meal in the air, and the use of perfectly formed ears of corn from prior harvests. If all the ceremonies are performed properly, and if the gods of fertility continue to be pleased, the seeds will sprout and the crops will surely grow well.

At the beginning of this planting season a few months before, Hosta and his father were aware that the rains had come when they were needed and that the clouds performed perfectly. So did their village Sun Watcher who then went to the Crier Chief and gave him the word that the next day would be perfect for the planting to take place.

At sunrise the next morning each farmer was anxious to begin work in his fields. Along with his favorite digging stick, each of the men carried a pouch which was made from the entire skin of a fawn with the head and legs still intact. The very best kernels of last years' corn harvest had been shucked from the cobs that had been carefully stored over the past winter where they remained safe from any dampness, rodents, or weevils. The seeds were then very carefully placed in the fawn-skin pouch. As each man left his home, women of the household poured bowls of water over his head as a symbolic gesture signifying their hope that the rains would come when they were needed. As additional offerings to the gods of germination, each farmer carried a smaller pouch of corn meal along with several prayer sticks.

When Hosta and his father, whose name is Koya, reached their field, both immediately attempted to locate its exact center. Hosta then backed away from his father and observed the next series of events as he had for as long as he could remember. Next year, he would be allowed to help his father perform these preparatory rituals because he had recently completed training which would allow him to share in this great honor. Hosta watched as his father punched four holes in the soft dirt each about a foot deep. The first hole was always made north of center, the second hole directly west, the third to the south, and another hole to the east. Yet another hole was made west of the first hole and lastly one was made on the eastern side of the southern hole. These represented the sky and the lower regions, all of which are important symbols to these early farmers.

Hosta watched his father closely but said nothing. In the center of the space made by the six holes Koya knelt slowly and faced to the east. He took a pinch of corn meal from his pouch and painted a cross with it on the ground. While muttering a simple prayer, which Hosta recited quietly to himself, he slipped one his prayer sticks in the center of the cross and sprinkled it with corn meal. Next he rose to his feet and opened the bag of seed corn and carefully selected six grains of corn, each a different color—yellow, blue, red, white, black, and white speckled with black. Returning now to the center of the field, he knelt once again and this time faced north and again began to chant. At the right moment in his prayers, Koya dropped four yellow kernels in the northern hole. Shifting to the west, four of the blue kernels were dropped in their holes. The chant continued as he placed red kernels in the southern hole, white to the east, speckled corn in those representing the sky regions, and lastly the black grains were placed in the hole representing the lower regions.

With this intricate planting ceremony now over, Koya covered each of the holes and mounded the earth. He then turned toward Hosta, and without saying a word, Hosta joined his father where both of them began planting four longer rows, each in a line representing the four compass directions. They first started to the north, then west, south, and lastly to the east. Their field was quite large and it took the better part of the afternoon to complete their planting.

At the end of this long day of ceremony and hard work, Hosta and his father quietly returned to their home for dinner and then could do nothing more during a four-day waiting period. Nothing more could be done in the fields until the four days passed. During this time Hosta and Koya said a number of additional ritual prayers and placed offerings at various shrines around their home. Certain foods were forbidden to be eaten during this time and the men had to avoid trading, gambling, and other pleasurable activities as well.

The remaining planting continued hurriedly after the four-day period ended. Every available hand participated in the remaining planting activities. Hosta, his father, and all able-bodied men of the villages worked in their fields and the women and girls brought food, water, and other needed supplies into the fields. Work began each day at sunrise and continued until the sun set.

The beans and squash were also planted at this time, although the holes were not dug as deeply nor was there much ceremony associated with this activity. At some times the corn, beans, and squash were planted in separate fields but most often everything is planted together in the same field. Girls are sometimes allowed to plant seeds along with the men and boys, and they consider it a great honor to be asked to help.

Soon after the planting was over, all family members awaited the coming of the gentle spring rains. These "female" rains would last for several days. They are not like the much more aggressive "male" rains that will come later in the summer.

Hosta and his family have been farming this land for several hundred years. They have developed into excellent farmers, and are extremely proud of their efforts. Throughout the summer all the men of each village will work their fields and watch their crops of corn, beans, and squash mature and grow. Every day just as the sun begins to rise, they will come into the fields and using their favorite digging sticks work hard at chopping weeds or simply loosening the soil from around their plants. Even when there are no weeds to pull, or no real work to do, they will still come to the fields and walk among these wonderful living things acting more like companions than serious workers.

On this particular day, about two months after all planting was complete, many things have changed for Hosta and his family. He is back in the fields today and takes time to look down and observe an incredible green shoot which is rising from the soil beneath his feet. Although he doesn't think much about it, this fragile seedling is largely responsible for all human life in this region of the world. The plant is called corn, or maize, and it came to this place from the south beginning its highly evolutionary life as a close relative of the many varieties of grass plants that grow throughout the world.

About six thousand years ago, this wild grass was cultivated by people in the Tehuacan Valley of present-day Mexico. Over a long period of time and largely because of human cultivation, this plant changed greatly. It developed a tight husk that wrapped more and more tightly around the seed-bearing cob. As this happened, the plant could no longer sow its own seeds. Only through human intervention when the husks were removed and the dried kernels were planted in the soil was this plant able to survive and continue its evolutionary development. Within a few thousand years, this remarkable plant formed a unique partnership with mankind as people became so accustomed to eating corn and preparing it in a variety of ways, that life itself revolved around the planting, the cultivating, the harvesting, and the storage of this hearty grain. A mutual dependence between man and corn allowed human populations to grow in numbers, and as they did, a migration of peoples spread northward.

Corn was to become one of the staple ingredients of life itself in this area of southwestern Colorado, as elsewhere. But alone, it was not sufficient to ensure a complete or nourishing diet. Corn is an excellent source of carbohydrates but lacks one of the vital amino acids which is needed to produce protein. It is an effective staple only when consumed in combination with other crops like beans or squash, and of the two, beans were by far the most important because they contain essential protein that is required for a healthy and balanced diet.

Like all members of his family, Hosta has a deep love and respect for the land, and for farming which makes the land productive and life itself possible. Even after the crops are harvested in the fall, he will come back to the land and work in this field, doing little more than removing any rocks or wind-blown debris that might clutter the place.

In early spring new land will continually be cleaned as these farmers have come to understand that these fields can support their farming efforts only for so many seasons. Low-growing shrubs, sagebrush, and other groundcovers must be dug up or pulled out to make new planting fields. Stone axes are used to cut out small trees and larger ones are set on fire and then removed. All throughout the region, smoke can be seen rising from nearly every direction. Fires will continue smoldering throughout the cool and damp spring until planting begins. These fields are in common ownership of the village and are allotted to groups of families known as clans. Each clan in turn provides a household with a number of fields that may grow or shrink in size depending on the clan's individual needs. As long as the land is farmed and properly taken care of, it will remain with the household forever. If the land is neglected or a household dies out, the fields may ultimately be reassigned to other households within the village.

During the growing season, none of these fields will ever be left unattended. Even at night, young men and boys will take turns watching the fields. It is especially important now, during the early growing season, when rabbits and squirrels might eat all of the shoots and crows or ravens might pull up the tender young plants. It would not take long for an entire field to be ruined, so the men and boys take turns at keeping watch over their precious growing crops.

The field in which Hosta now stands was planted in late April just after all frost had vanished and the soil was dry enough to work. The primary tool of these farmers was the digging stick, that is, a slender hardwood stick with one end sharpened into a chisel-like blade. Some of the fancier digging sticks have a rounded knob on the top, and sometimes near the base a prong sticks out so the farmer's foot can help force the blade deep down into the soil. Stone blades are sometimes attached to the digging sticks, making the tool useful for many important chores like turning up the soil and chopping out weeds.

Not far from this place, Hosta was born, and today he stands just a little under five feet eight inches tall, which is slightly taller than the average man. Unlike most men who are heavyset, Hosta has a slender yet mature build. He has long dark hair and dark tanned skin. He is the oldest child in his family and came into this world with the able assistance of his maternal grandmother who still lives with the family in a small village nearby. His entrance into the world was without much effort, for his mother is a strong and active woman with great physical strength and stamina. Immediately after he was born, Hosta was thoroughly bathed and then dried by being rubbed all over with juniper ashes. This would protect him from witches and any other evil influence that might harm him. He was then placed on a bed of warm sand and a perfectly formed ear of corn was set down beside him. For twenty days Hosta and his mother were kept confined in their house and away from the strong light of the early spring days. Every fifth day his mother's hair was washed with yucca suds and she bathed in water in which juniper twigs had been thoroughly boiled. At sunrise on the twenty-first day of Hosta's life, his head was washed and he was taken away by his father's mother to a high place not far from the village. A few prayers were said and she then dedicated this child to Father Sun. Each relative on both his mother's and father's side gave a name to the newborn son, who received nearly a dozen names in all. One name, that of his mother's great-grandfather, has won out over the years.

For all of the months of that spring and summer, Hosta spent his life on a cradle board. Before about 900 A.D. his people used a very practical soft padded cradle on which they carried their young. For some reason, which no one has yet adequately explained, the type of cradle used changed rather dramatically. This new carrier was nothing more than a thin and smooth wooden board on which a child was bound with folds of cotton cloth or buckskin along with a lacing of strings. The baby's soft and pliable head rested on the board, and the back of the head gradually began to flatten until it took on the shape of the board. There was no physical damage and this change in the shape of the head had no negative effect on the child other than the distinctive appearance one would have throughout life.

Depending on how long the baby remained strapped to the cradle board, the skull could change in shape to the point where the back of the head pressed out to bulge over the ears. The brain can easily adjust to this gradual change, and the child will suffer no ill effects. Some of the people in Hosta's village have a tremendous deformity, as their head is nearly as wide as it is long. Some have suggested that this change may have been brought about because people came in contact with others who had similar deformities and that it simply became a fashion, or craze, or a kind of beauty fad. Whatever the reason, the cradle board did have many practical advantages for a mother and it made child care somewhat easier. The board was often carried on the mother's back as she went about her daily tasks. From time to time she might hang the board and baby on a nearby tree or roof pole. Because the child is firmly placed on the board it is in no danger of rolling off or being pecked at by the constant hordes of turkeys that are found roaming throughout the villages.

The baby is taken off the board from time to time when a juniper bark pad, which serves as a diaper, needs to be changed. At about age one, the baby is taken off the cradle board completely and it must learn to walk or it will be returned to the board until it is ready to learn to walk. Hosta took to walking quickly and the back of his head is flat, but not nearly as flat as other boys in his village.

Because it is nearing summer, Hosta wears little except for a loin cloth and sandals, both of which have been woven from yucca fibers. Until a few seasons ago, Hosta wore no clothing at all and still likes to walk around without anything on his feet. He prefers the more intimate feeling when the sandy soil creeps up between his toes.

This young man would be considered quite handsome if that were an important matter. His dark and deep-set eyes added warmth to his broad smile that came easily to his smooth and unblemished face. He is the oldest of three living siblings, having both a younger brother and sister. His mother, who is called Say, had given birth to two other sons, both of whom had not survived their first winters. Hosta was too young to remember either of these boys, but was told that not even the medicine men were able to keep the witches from taking them. Now, with his father still missing and perhaps unlikely ever to return, Hosta has accepted his proper role as responsible for the family and is greatly torn between this loyalty and the feelings he has been having difficulty ridding himself of over the past several weeks.

The intense sun is now almost directly overhead and Hosta is getting hungry. None of his fellow farm workers take any nourishment in the morning, and many of the men are now on their way home to eat their first meal of the day with their families. Others, like Hosta, have brought something to eat and are now walking across the fields to seek whatever shade they can find.

Hosta walks slowly away from many of the others in order to find a comfortable spot under a juniper tree at the edge of a field. Just before sitting down, Ika comes running toward him.

"Hosta," Ika shouted, "Mind if I join you?"

Although Hosta really wanted to be alone in order to savor and work out his troubling thoughts, he waves his right arm in the air welcoming his best friend to come over and join him.

"Going to be another warm afternoon," Ika says as he drops his digging stick and quickly sits on the ground in front of Hosta.

"Yah," is the simple reply.

"What's wrong? You seem quiet again today as you were last week," Ika observed, looking directly into Hosta's eyes. Hosta breaks eye contact, looks down at the ground, picks up a twig, and begins making circles in the dry reddish-brown soil.

"Just . . . I dunno . . . just thinking about stuff," Hosta says.

"Like, what stuff, is it your uncle giving you a hard time again, or what?" his friend probes, trying to break through a side of Hosta he has seldom seen before. It was usually Ika who needed a friend's shoulder to cry on. With the roles now reversed, Ika was suggesting some discomfort and concern.

"Naw, nothing like that Ika, it's just . . ."

"Just what?"

Hosta has to make a decision. Should he confide in his best friend about this rather delicate subject, or just pass it off and change subjects? Hosta drew a couple more circles in the dirt and then tosses the twig to his right.

"You gotta keep this just between us," Hosta says now looking straight into his friend's eyes. Ika says nothing, but moves uncomfortably around his small patch of shade preparing to listen to whatever his friend might now begin to reveal.

"You remember the planting ceremony up at Chichta," Hosta nearly whispers.

"Sure, we were all there," Ika observed as though this was hardly something anyone would forget so quickly.

"Do you remember the girl they call Katti? The one whose eyes are slightly crossed and who carried one of the food baskets for the Koshare?" Hosta asks.

"Sure, I remember her. She's the one who has a younger brother who kept running around getting into . . ." Ika stops in mid-sentence as it becomes clear that his best friend was not really interested in knowing about these observations. Something else is happening, and a sudden recognition of Hosta's real interest in this girl is becoming obvious to Ika. "Why do you ask?"

Hosta looks down to the ground and takes a deep breath before continuing. "I cannot keep her out of my mind," he says slowly. "During the day in the fields, at night when the night sounds come, I can hardly think of anything else but her. I want to talk with her and just be near to her," Hosta says with a sincerity uncharacteristic of this sometimes playful young man.

Just as this conversation is about to continue, a rustling of branches and the crisp sound of breaking twigs is heard. The two young men look to the west and see one of the women from their village walking slowly toward them. Her head is bent to the ground and every now and then she stoops to pick up something. Because this is June, the uncultivated portions of the ground are covered with flowers of all kinds and the women often walked for miles picking stems, leaves, flowers, or berries of many varieties of plants. These items will be used not only for food, but for important medicinal and ceremonial purposes as well. Even the fruit of the prickly pear is eaten along with its leaves. The beautiful and waxy flowers and stems of the yucca plant have many valuable uses. The search would also produce lily bulbs, wild onion plants, Beeweed, and sumac berries. Every woman knows and understands the value of each seed, root, bulb, or berry that grows in this part of their world. The women will walk all over the land throughout the summer looking for a remarkable variety of food supplements, flavorings, and items for healing.

The woman from the village passes some distance away, having not even noticed the two young men talking under the shade of their tree. This brief interruption allows Hosta and his friend a chance to gather their individual thoughts before beginning the conversation again.

"What do you want to do?" Ika asks his friend.

"I don't know. I must first talk with my uncle. Maybe he can give me some ideas. And then I suppose I'll need to talk with Mom too."

The young lady Hosta is troubled over is equally distracted. At the same time the two young men are sitting in the shade near their fields, Katti is helping her mother with the daily chores. Katti is a sturdy young lady with short dark hair. Her eyes are slightly crossed, a family characteristic much in evidence near the place where her family lived not more than a mile from Hosta's small village. Katti stands very straight but her excellent posture will probably not last long because of the demanding chores she is performing, and will continue to perform throughout her life. Just after the men leave for the fields, Katti, her mother, and younger sister—now in her seventh season—go on their daily walk to the springs to collect water. They carry large pottery jars that will be filled with the cool and sweet spring water, using long-handled ladles. As they walk toward the spring, Katti and her mother keep their eyes lowered to the ground just in case some wild onion or other important plant might be found along the way and taken back home.

As they walk together, Katti's thoughts wander back to the early spring planting ceremony. It was there that she had caught the eye of a rather handsome young man whose name was given to her by a friend. She remembers having seen him many times before and cannot understand why this most recent encounter keeps him in her mind. Perhaps it is because she felt something more than his mere physical presence.

"Look there," Katti's mother shouts to her. Not ten yards ahead a Beeweed plant was in flower. The Beeweed plant is an erect annual herb that grows up to three feet tall along the edges of washes or streams and in the sandy soil of this region. It is a wonderfully useful plant. Multiple clusters of about three leaflets grow on the lower part of the stem, and toward the top of the plant and close to the flowers are single leaves about an inch long. The pink and purple flowers have long stamens that grow in round clusters. Seed pods extend downward from the stems and enclose small pea-like seeds.

Both Katti and her mother walk up to the plant and begin picking its leaves and pulling selected stems from the plant. The women work in silence at this useful and pleasant activity. The plant is a storehouse of useful things. The leaves can be used to flavor a variety of stews, and the seeds are gathered to be stored. If enough of them are accumulated over the summer they will be ground and made into mush or bread. The medicine men also use the leaves for healing and to make a special tea that is very useful in treating common stomachaches. But it is the stems that Katti and her mother are really after. They will collect enough of them so that they can be boiled down into a dark brown and sticky mass. The end result will later be whetted down with water and used as a pigment for painting their pottery. Beeweed turns black when it is applied to pottery and then fired.

After this brief and satisfying diversion, the women call out for young Massay who has managed to wander away from them and is now kicking at a small ant-hill she has found not far away. The three walk toward the springs to finish the hardest task of the day, which is to load and carry precious water back home.

Katti and her mother scoop nearly five gallons of water into the first jar, and nearly as much into a second jar. Both women have brought a small pad made of yucca fibers that has been woven into a large doughnut shape. They place these under their water jars and then lift them both onto their heads. The pads will help balance their incredibly heavy burden and at the same time will keep their callused heads from cracking their precious water jars.

This difficult task now over, the journey back home begins and Katti can focus on her individual thoughts. The day is growing warm, especially now with the sun directly overhead, and it is good that a gentle breeze occasionally washes across their faces as they walk towards home.

Katti says little on the journey. Although this is not uncommon, her thoughts of late had been taking her to places and things she has only recently began to imagine. But it is not her place to initiate any direct contact with the young man called Hosta.

The future holds much uncertainty for her on this warm and pleasant day, and her thoughts continue to drift throughout the day and evening.

CHAPTER
two

Our day didn't begin as early as we had planned. In fact, we were both awakened by voices and the sounds of activity not far away.

Diane and I had rented a motor home in Durango the day before, after having driven to the area from our home in Boulder. We arrived in Durango at mid-afternoon and spent the better part of an hour on an important telephone conference call by way of our cellular phone. Diane and I were involved in a company that was in the process of becoming publicly traded. After months of work by our partners who spent hundreds of hours with an army of accountants and attorneys, this was the critical day when we would confer with the underwriting firm and decide an initial offering price for the stock that would, we hoped, begin trading in a matter of days. We both felt some sense of guilt at not being in the center of this interesting and important activity by joining our partners at the meeting being held concurrently in New York City and Minneapolis.

But our plans to drive to the Four Corners area had already been made and we weren't about to change them. We drove to a city park in Durango, and parked along the banks of the Animas River which flows through town. We were soon connected to our partners who were engaged in a conference call with our investment advisors. It was with much anticipation and some anxiety that we joined in with a lively discussion about the state of the market and our chances for success in bringing forward the public offering. After half an hour or so we all agreed to end this call and discuss the situation among ourselves with a separate call. Within the hour we had all agreed to move forward and conclude this portion of a rather important business matter.

We then picked up the motor home, and drove to our lot at the Indian Camp Ranch where we set up a little campsite under some of the juniper and pinyon trees. From our vantage point, we could look directly south toward Shiprock that is some 60 miles distant and in the State of New Mexico. Toward the south and east we had a great view of the multi-colored rock strata of Mesa Verde. Looming south and west was the "Sleeping Ute" Mountain. We were in a beautiful setting and, all in all, it had been quite an interesting day. We had a quick and simple dinner before sitting briefly under an incredibly starry sky where I watched the clouds chase a bright and nearly full moon. I was tired but elated, and then retired for the night.

Now that we were hearing voices not far away, we eagerly got up and walked over to the site.

"Good morning," Jerry said as we approached.

"Hi, Jerry," I replied. "Meet Diane. And Di, these two hard working young ladies are Kelly McAndrews and Kay Barnett," I said.

Greetings were exchanged all around and we got caught up on the current state of our project activities. Earlier in the week, Jerry, Kelly, and Kay had staked out a one-meter-wide by ten-meter-long section across the area they had augered earlier in the spring. It was across this section that a structure was likely located beneath the soil. The team had begun digging a trench along the lines staked out, and they had already excavated down about a foot or so. At the northern end of the trench, a number of white stones could be seen and the young ladies were scraping away some of the loose soil near them.

"That could be the beginning of a bench or a wall although it's a bit early to tell," Jerry told us as we watched this current work. "We'll need to move some more dirt here and there," he pointed in our direction as we awaited instructions on how we could join in.

After getting an orientation on the current level of activity from the team, Diane and I were each invited to grab a trench digger. Under Jerry's supervision, we eagerly began digging away.

Working an archaeological site may seem like a rather romantic activity. In fact, it is, but it's also a lot of hard work. Near the surface, the soil here is loose and sandy and not very hard to scrape away. About half a foot down, the dirt becomes quite a bit more solid, and it takes a good deal of muscle to break through the compacted soil.

The digging can't be done fast, because part of what you're doing is looking for things that might randomly show up as you go along. Ceramic pieces can appear along with pieces of flint, bone, charcoal, and any number of interesting things. When this happens, you tend to dig a little slower, looking for what other things might be nearby and try to make sure nothing important or significant gets chopped up.

After enough material is loosened away from where you're digging, it is scooped into buckets and yet another physical challenge awaits. Not far from the trench, an upright triangular device known as a "shaker" has been set up. It looks something like a small teepee and in the center of the three-legged device hangs a wooden frame suspended from the top. In the bottom of the frame is wire mesh made with about a quarter-inch grid. You either dump a bucketful of dirt into the frame, or shovel it in from a wheelbarrow. Then you take hold of the wooden frame and begin rocking it back and forth and side to side, sifting through the sand and rock or dirt you've mined from the earth.

You search through the stones and break up the clumps of dirt and look for anything that appears a bit unusual. Running your hands over the rock and dirt and stones, you might find additional pieces of pottery, lithic material, bone, and a variety of interesting and often astounding things. This is the romantic part of your search—the quest for things undiscovered—and it's quite like a treasure hunt because you never know what you might run across.

The digging process is not only physical, but mentally stimulating as well. Earth is moved in one or two meter sections at a time, to a depth of about 20 centimeters. Artifacts found in each section are carefully identified by type, and then placed into paper bags for cataloguing and later analysis. While all of this activity goes forward, one of the team members is keeping a site log of the dig. From time to time a transit is used to record the precise depth and exact location of the materials recovered. When noteworthy items are recovered, a photograph is often taken right where the object is found for exact documentation and for use in a follow-up report that will be produced.

For Diane and me, all of this activity was quite exciting and new. The rest of the team took things in stride, but whenever something interesting or unusual turned up, it's a completely new discovery and everyone shares in the excitement. Even Jerry Fetterman, who has been doing this kind of work for over twenty years, will become quite animated when an interesting artifact or discovery is made.

Cotton-white clouds began to build around noontime and the team took a break to sit and enjoy lunch. The day was warm, and the sun intense. Lunch was taken in the shade of the trees surrounding our site and talk was centered on the emerging kiva we were working on. A kiva is nothing more than a dwelling that, over several hundred years, evolved in many interesting and important ways.

When man first moved throughout this land in prehistoric times, shelter first consisted of nothing more than an open cave or rock outcropping. Adopting a more permanent living area was of great importance in the evolution of man in this area of the world. Life in caves could never have been very comfortable. With heavy rains in the summer, and deep snows and bitter cold temperatures of winter, populations were always in a survival mode seeking such fundamental things as warmth and shelter from the elements. Not until a more permanent form of shelter was developed would populations be able to grow in size and gain stability.

Among the earliest dwellings in this region were pit houses that were nothing more than shelters partially dug into the ground with some form of protective covering above. The portion dug below ground consisted of a shallow pit two or more feet in depth and from ten to twenty feet in diameter. Some later plaster walls were found to have evidence of over-painted decoration similar to petroglyphs and pictographs found on rock walls throughout the Four Corners area. Some other structures suggested that stones were used to shore up the walls that might otherwise have tended to cave in.

On the floor of the pit house four holes were dug and four wooden forked posts slightly longer and higher than a man's head were set vertically into the holes. Now forming a large square, four slender logs were horizontally placed in the forks of these posts that together made a square framework and a structure on which smaller poles could be rested. These more slender poles were set into a framework every foot or so around the single room. Even smaller poles were then placed across the flat top portion that helped to enclose this basic structure. To this frame, reeds, brush, bark, or even coarse grass was lashed in an attempt to fortify and seal the unit. After basically weaving twigs and poles to the roof, several inches of earth were placed on top. A small hatchway was left in the center of the roof that served not only as the access to the house but also a chimney. This opening was usually equipped with a ladder, again made of wooden poles with several cross-members.

In the center of the room and directly below the opening was a fire pit. And since both room and fire pit needed some kind of ventilation, a tunnel was usually dug through the south wall of the pit house and tunneled up to the surface. The main purpose of the tunnel was for ventilation, although at times this tunnel served as an additional entrance to the house. Over time, this tunnel evolved into a second room, always smaller than the main living area, but in time it was also roofed in much the same manner as the larger pit house.

In some pit houses excavated over the past hundred years, these smaller antechambers are connected by a tunnel. One of the main reasons for this structural element was for fresh air circulation into the fire pit area of the main room. Most often a large stone slab is also found just in front of the tunnel to the antechamber. It served as a deflector keeping fresh air from blowing out the fire and in the winter helping to prevent cold air from constantly drifting across the people who were sleeping on the floor.

The importance of the pit house cannot be underestimated. Its use and development had far-reaching impact on the development of family life and other human development. Stable families were not able to flourish when people lived in rather haphazard groups seeking shelter with others in caves or rock shelters. Having a single enclosed dwelling unit began to change all of this. As families were able to grow, both in size and varying degrees of separated domestic responsibility, the basic pit house structure itself changed in many significant ways.

With agriculture becoming increasing important as the primary source of food and sustenance, the need for and use of storage devices increased. Not only did this require-ment lead to the development of ceramics for use as storage containers, but also the need for specific storage areas for the foodstuffs produced. In time, the people built slab-lined storage rooms adjacent to their pit houses. In the beginning these storage areas were rather small, but over time they gradually became larger until they too could be used as liv-ing areas. The floors of these storage rooms were built slightly below ground level and stone slabs were often used to line the walls of these pits. Part of the rooms was built of poles and an important natural material that would quickly become nearly impossible to live without—adobe.

Adobe is a rather simple product, being nothing more than a combination of earth, water, and a binder of some kind. Grass or dried hay served the purpose quite well. Because rocks are rather irregular in shape, and often require a great deal of physical preparation when used in construction, adobe is particularly useful because it can more easily be shaped or molded into manageable sizes. Later, the layering of adobe blocks one on top of the other became a significant change in the manner and method of architectural techniques. Its importance in providing man with shelter cannot be underestimated.

Another common feature of these early structures was a small hole that was dug into the floor of the house near the fire pit. This hole is called a "sipapu" and it serves as a symbolic entrance for the people into their Mother Earth. It was from this hole in the earth that man was able to enter into this world. The sipapu seems to be the symbolic high-way to the spirit world as well as to the world all people live in. This unique feature survives today as many of the mod-ern Pueblo Peoples have similar holes in the floors of modern-day kivas.

Over time, storage and living areas became more rectan-gular and the sides of the structures more vertical. Improved walls made it possible for more and more rooms to be joined together in long rows. As materials and techniques improved over time, the traditional pit house evolved into something quite different. Some of these pit house structures became deeper and gradually developed into rooms that served as a place for various ceremonial purposes. This evolution produced what we refer to as a kiva. It is the kiva, a mainly subterranean and circular room that is still used today by the present day Pueblo Indians of the American Southwest.

In ruins throughout the region, kivas come in all sizes. Some of them are huge like those that can be visited today at Chaco Canyon, or at the Aztec Ruins near Farmington, New Mexico. Several hundred people can participate in events and activities in these kivas although they certainly began as much smaller dwellings and evolved over time into what they are today.

In some transition period, the kiva became the ceremonial and dwelling place primarily inhabited by men. Women and children occupied the earliest kiva structures, but as more and more frequent structured ceremonial activities evolved, the kiva became more of a ritualistic sanctuary for men and boys. Women were not entirely excluded from kivas, but their participation and activities there were always regulated by the men.

As time went on, groups of individual pit houses grew in number and soon small enclaves of several different but usually related persons began to live in close proximity to one another. As storage rooms became larger, more building activity was taking place closer to the surface and underground living became less common. Clusters of people began living together, often building common areas between their individual dwellings. Plazas and pathways grew in importance and more elaborate structures were built for the community good. Some of these structures look like towers and they may have been used for protecting living areas from intruders or even enemies. The sociological progression of these prehistoric peoples is a fascinating story that has great usefulness in our gaining a better understanding of humankind and of human and social development. It is the location, discovery, and thoughtful interpretation of our shared human past that archaeology is all about.

While eating our lunches, we discussed some of what we were finding in our initial digging, including the fact that we had most likely encountered a typical Pueblo II (900–1150 A.D.) kiva structure. Also during our lunch hour a number of visitors dropped by to pay us a friendly visit. Just as we were finishing up and getting ready to head back to work, the most ubiquitous mode of travel in the southwestern United States drove up to the site. The pickup door screeched open, and out came Edmund—one of the Indian Camp Ranch workmen. The development was just about a year old, and a great deal of work was being done to improve its physical appearance and function as a residential development. Roads had been cut to each of the lots, and the necessary culverts, drainage ways, and fences were being worked on. Edmund had been hired by Archie Hanson to coordinate many of the contract laborers who were engaged in doing a variety of jobs. Edmund himself spent a lot of time at the stone quarry that was on the northwestern edge of the property. Many stone walls were being built along each of the access roads and along the culverts. It was heavy and backbreaking work not unlike that in which we were engaged.

Edmund is of Native American descent, although he is not related to the ancestral Pueblo people. He is a Navajo and lives on tribal land in Arizona not far from Indian Camp Ranch. Edmund is stocky like most Navajo men, stands about five foot eight, has dark skin, long dark hair, and other distinctive Indian facial features. He spoke slowly and softly and uttered a short greeting to Jerry, Kelly, Kay, and to us.

We went back to work while Edmund and Jerry chatted for a while about something or other. Because ours was not the only archaeological project in the process of being explored at the time, it was logical that Edmund and Jerry had reason to speak with one another about any number of things. Edmund and Jerry didn't visit long and Jerry came back to join us.

"Edmund says he found a nice stone ax head up where they're doing some stonework on Archie's lot," Jerry said as he peered into the growing hole we were digging. "Wants me to take a look at it."

"You find many of those around here?" I asked.

"Actually, quite a few, but it's always interesting to see some particularly nice ones, and Edmund says this one is quite nice," Jerry replied. "He might bring it down here later, if we don't find any bones here, that is."

"Why's that?", I asked.

"Well, the Navajo get kinda spooky about any dead bodies," Jerry said. "In fact we discovered a number of human remains up at Archie's site last year. Once we did and Edmund found out about it, he's never been back up there. Neither has any of his Navajo workers either," Jerry reported.

I recalled having read that many Native Americans have rather interesting and cautious views of the dead. There is both reverence and fear associated with death and dying. Ancestors are important and oftentimes worshipped, but bones of the dead and places were bodies might be buried don't seem to have much appeal for many Native American people.

"Think we'll find any dead bodies here?" Diane asked.

Both Kelly and Jerry said it couldn't be ruled out, and we shouldn't be surprised if we did.

"Do we have to stop digging if we find something like that?" Diane asked.

"No, but we'll certainly need to report anything we do find," Jerry said.

Under professional guidance and regulatory authority, any human remains uncovered while working on an archaeological project would not only need to be reported but ultimately sent to the Office of the State Archaeologist in Denver for disposal. This whole area has become one of great sensitivity in recent years and such outstanding organizations such as the Smithsonian Institution have been caught up in controversies related to the storage and disposition of the remains of Native American people. To us, it might not seem like any big deal, but in fact, one can learn to become quite sympathetic with the concerns expressed by Native Americans on this particular issue.

The next couple of hours consisted of digging, scooping, and hauling, along with screening and record-keeping. We had marked out the next level to be dug and were beginning to find more white stone layered one on top of the other just in front of the first set of stones we had uncovered. This second set of stonework, which was about a foot in front of, and a foot below the first stone wall, was the interior edge of the kiva and formed the top of a bench. This pattern was quite typical of kivas built in this area where the bench was used for setting down various objects, whether ceremonial or utilitarian. So far we had collected a number of small ceramic pieces, of both painted and unpainted pottery. Most of the unpainted pottery sherds we uncovered or screened out were "corrugated" or had the distinctive appearance of being hand made. Individual coils of clay had been pinched together as the sidewalls of the pottery vessel were being formed between the fingers of some ancient craftsperson.

In addition, a large number of lithic materials were being found rather randomly as we dug. These flint-like pieces are usually small, but quite sharp and very capable of cutting your skin. None of the pieces uncovered so far looked anything like an arrowhead, and were probably the remains of the process of making stone points or arrowheads that is called "knapping." Knapping is done when larger pieces of flint material are worked with stone tools. As the stones are knocked against the flint, various flakes chip off the main body of flint and the material is routinely discarded.

The day before Diane and I arrived, one of the team had found a portion of a clay gaming token. It was already bagged and catalogued and I was in desperate search for more of them—looking for one that might even be intact. It is always easy finding pieces of something, but much more difficult to locate anything whole and in good condition. That is always the hope and desire of an amateur digger. It is much more common, however, to find just bits and pieces of things.

The warm afternoon wore on and every now and then one of the fluffy-white clouds offered needed relief from the sun. We decided that building a sun screen over the excavation might be a good idea and a worthwhile project to be done before starting any more digging the next day.

At about half past four, Jerry and the crew decided to think about calling it a day. Tools needed to be put away, the rest of the data needed to be recorded, and the site generally needed to be cleaned up. Diane, however, seemed not the least interested in calling it quits. She was working intently at the bottom level of the kiva, seemed to not be losing any steam, and was quite content to continue getting filthy.

This is the woman who brought a box-load of books with her along with a couple of our most comfortable reclining lawn chairs from home. Initially, this whole business was sort of "my deal" and Diane thought it might just be fun to come camping with me for a week. I think she envisioned herself reading a few summer novels as she didn't initially express much interest in taking hold of a shovel, trowel, or wheelbarrow. But this stuff becomes somewhat hypnotic once you get into it. Especially when you start finding things and the hole in the ground takes to take on some shape and definition. It isn't long before you begin to sense the presence of human activity in times long ago and try to imagine what life might have been like before motor homes, pickup trucks, and pay-per-view TV.

"You gonna quit sometime soon?" I asked.

"Well, sure, but just let me finish up this section," Diane replied still full of steam.

"O.K., but I sure could use a shower and a beer," I said.

"You'll get your shower and beer, 'cause I need both too, so just hang on," was her reply.

Jerry, Kay, and Kelly bid farewell for the day and said they'd be back the next morning bright and early. Before they left they wanted to make sure they weren't going off and leaving a couple amateur yet eager diggers to mess up their well-organized and efficiently running project. They gave us specific instructions on what more could be done without doing irreparable damage; so we worked on for another hour or so with Diane being by far the best and most efficient worker.

The absolute best part of the day came next. We didn't have a lot of water on board the motor home, just enough to do the dishes and flush the toilet a time or two. And we didn't want to keep breaking camp to drive into town for more water if we could avoid it. The very accommodating people at the Crow Canyon Archaeological Center invited us to use one of their bathrooms that was equipped with a shower. What a gift that was for us as we each literally peeled away our clothing that early evening. We were covered from head to toe in dirt—the really grimy stuff—and there is nothing like the feel of warm water and good sudsy soap helping remove a couple layers of the soggy gunk from all over. The shower water ran red-brown for each of us. We were both quite a mess. Toweling off and getting into recently laundered clean clothes was a nearly religious experience.

We went back to our campsite, had a couple of cold beers, and a pleasant and simple dinner before watching a typical yet incredible Southwestern summer sunset. Diane went in to wash up a few items and I was left to think about this incredible woman I married nearly 30 years ago.

We were both undergraduate students in radio and television at Iowa State University in Ames, Iowa. At the time, I managed the campus radio station that was housed in the men's dormitory on campus. In the early 1960s you simply couldn't have men and women living in the same dormitory and it was an eventful time when I decided to add a few female disc jockeys to our all-male staff. Diane was one of the first applicants interviewed and was immediately given an air shift.

We were married in 1965 and she had another year of college to finish. I went into graduate school in Journalism and Mass Communication and worked as a teaching assistant before joining the faculty full-time after graduation. From there we moved to Des Moines where I became involved in the advertising and public relations business. But our true love was always radio, and in 1975 we purchased a daytime-only AM radio station in Boulder, Colorado. By then we had two kids, AnneMarie and Rob, whom we uprooted and moved west. Through a lot of hard work and a dedicated and talented staff, we were able to create an AM and FM operation in Boulder that served the greater Denver area. We sold the stations in 1988 and Diane decided to enroll in graduate school at the University of Colorado.

Diane is a remarkable person. She is the love of my life as well as my best friend, and the best friend of a number of other people as well. Sensitive and caring, she has a wide variety of interests and a deep curiosity and insight on many things. One particular interest led her to graduate school as an Art History major with particular emphasis and interest in Asian art. She was even invited to teach Asian Art History in the Art History Department at the University of Colorado, which I believe she enjoyed very much. I laughed to myself as I recalled this day of digging together in a hot, dirty hole in the ground and thought again what a lucky guy I was to have a companion so interested and willing to participate in many of the rather strange and uncommon things I seem to get involved with.

Earlier than normal for me, we both went to bed tired, a tiny bit stiff, but wonderfully clean, well refreshed, and satisfied from a very full and rewarding day.

CHAPTER
three

At night, the witches come out.

Witches are the epitome of evil and have a single mission: to provide disharmony, chaos, and even destroy people. They possess very special powers and cause not only sickness, but can stop the rains from coming when they are most needed. They can also completely destroy a good harvest of crops. It has even been told that witches are capable of making both the sun and the moon completely disappear from Father Sky. There are many stories that have been continuously told about the awesome power of witches. These stories are passed down by the people in order to warn others about the evil that witches bring.

To these prehistoric people everything is a great mystery. The sun rising each morning and setting each evening is unsettling and disconcerting to them. Great powers exist in the universe—life, death, wind, rain, everything that is known or felt is a complete mystery.

Of all the powers known it is the sun that evokes the most interest and concern. The sun and sky are Father to all the people. He gives life and light and is perhaps the most important external force that anyone can experience. Next, there is Mother Earth. She nurtures the people and has tremendous power just as the sun has. From Mother Earth come water, food, shelter, and every important tangible thing that anyone could need or want.

Control of Father Sky and Mother Earth rests with the gods. In addition to the gods of sun and earth, there are gods who control the rains, the growth of plants, the health and well-being of the people. Communication between these gods and man can be accomplished through priests who know how to call upon various gods for special favors or for knowledge about a wide variety of things that not only might be interesting but often of vital importance to understand more fully.

When things become particularly problematic, medicine men can also be called upon to help in making sure that things never get out of control or that a proper balance of forces is maintained. This ancient concept of harmony and balance is important to all the people and is somewhat reminiscent of the Chinese theory of yin and yang—equally strong but opposite forces of good and evil, strength and weakness, even life or death. Achieving harmony is what the shamans, or medicine men, attempt to provide and their work is often complex.

When people are in need of help, for whatever reason, the priests and medicine men are available to assist in the understanding or acceptance of whatever needs to be resolved. Every act of nature that affects people, every illness or evil can be explained in some way, which is where the tremendous body of Native American legends and myths have come from. In the constant telling and re-telling of these myths and legends, the unexplainable is explained. This process is not religion per se, but a complex system of attempting to understand and explain how man can seek ways to satisfy his need to comprehend and understand complex issues for which there were rarely answers—no matter how sophisticated man's level of technology or science might be.

Witches create and thrive on disharmony. Because a witch can live right among the people, they can dwell in a single family or village and they might even take the form of one of your closest friends, a neighbor, or even a member of your own family. Not all witches take on the human form, however. Sometimes they take the form of a dog, or an owl, or coyote. Only medicine men can recognize witches and only they can counteract the evil that might be perpetrated on good people. Only a shaman has the same power that a witch has and only he can intervene to prevent evil, illness, or even death.

Because you never know who the witches are, you must constantly remain on alert. You must remain cautious about offending anyone because you might inadvertently create certain disaster for yourself. Because you can never be sure about such things, all people are taught to be suspicious of any unusual actions by the people around them. If someone in a village becomes unusually unhappy, or jealous, or if someone begins to roam around at night—especially near the house where someone is ill or recently died—that person might be accused of witchcraft and would immediately be shunned and perhaps even driven away from the village. If other people begin to suffer because of illness, or if the rains were never to come when they should during the growing season, or if other terrible things happen, the person accused of being a witch will be severely punished. It is not uncommon that if things were to get worse, the person accused of witchcraft might even have to be executed.

Hosta is well aware of these things and has to be cautious about his current state of mind, and particularly his actions. Because his father is missing and might never return, Hosta's family and most other members of the village are aware of the stress this is causing. They would be understanding of his current state of mind but it would be dangerous if others knew about the additional burdens now plaguing his mind. Whenever troubling thoughts concerning the young lady he has become infatuated with came into his thoughts, Hosta tried to remain calm and cautious so that his behavior did not seem strange enough that others might take notice.

On this particular moonlit night, Hosta has just finished a quiet and satisfying dinner with his family. Say prepared her own special cornbread for which she was somewhat famous. In addition, there was roasted deer meat that had been boiled with some freshly picked herbs. Tonight there was even a pot of fresh greens that had been mixed with beans and flavored with some wild onion. A pot of thin corn gruel that served as a tea had also been prepared. Corn is the backbone of nearly every meal. It is not only the most plentiful foodstuff but one of the most versatile as well.

The grinding of corn is usually done by the younger women who use smooth flat stones that are slanted toward small bins. At the lower end of this stone, which is called a *metate*, is a clean adobe basin that helps gather the freshly ground corn meal. Kneeling at the other end, the woman places dried corn kernels on the flat stone and takes up another, and smaller, flat stone called a *mano*. Sliding the mano back and forth on the metate for several hours is backbreaking work, but the women have been doing this essential kind of labor for centuries. Younger men will sometimes help, although their generosity often takes the form of singing festive tunes to help pass the time and take some of the drudgery out of the task.

Corn meal can be prepared in a wide variety of ways. The most simple method involves adding water to the meal and then cooking the batter on a hot stone. Sometimes juniper ash is added to the batter to give it a bluish appearance. Corn dough can also be rolled in corn husks and baked on the hot coals of a fire. Or larger cakes might be baked in hot ovens. When both coarse and fine corn meals are combined and rolled into little balls, they are boiled in a pot of stew resulting in a simple but tasty dumpling.

Say's specialty is a corn bread she helps to sweeten with her own saliva. She takes some fine corn meal and chews on it while she works. Her saliva helps change the starch of the corn meal into sugar and when it is combined with the other batter, rolled up into corn leaves and boiled, a sweet corn bread is the result.

Because Hosta is now the man of the family, as soon as his mother places the boiling pots on the ground, he takes a small pinch of each of the items from their cooking pots and tosses them into the fire. This act is a symbolic offering to the gods and not until the ritual is completed can everyone begin to eat. For a time after Koya had not returned home, Hosta felt quite awkward performing this essential ritual. But some time had now passed and he performed this duty eagerly.

Tonight's meal is being shared by Hosta's extended family that includes his grandfather and grandmother, two aunts, and a widowed lady from the village who takes turns dining with various members of the village. Everyone dips their fingers into each of the pots. Chunks of the meat are picked out, and since the food is quite hot, they will often use corn bread on which to rest the steaming meat before chewing it. Bones are gnawed on and then simply dropped back into one of the pots as fingers were needed for another item. Dunking bread into the thick soups and stews is one of the more common methods of eating.

Grandmother has lost most of her teeth over the years, so she has her own bowl in which she tosses bread, meat, and broth. She drinks the mixture quickly using both hands to hold the bowl. Stein-like mugs hold the corn tea and Say had set a couple of her most ornately decorated pottery ladles into the soupy mixture so all could share in the meal she had been proud to prepare.

The family speaks little during the meal. The food is the center of attention and activity. The only noises that can be heard are the licking of fingers and the loud smacking of lips, offering the cook an expression of great appreciation and satisfaction. Hosta recalls his father making the most hearty of noises when he ate and uttering deep rumbling belches after a meal. This was not an unpleasant sound and it gave Say great satisfaction in knowing that her efforts were very much appreciated by her husband, and there could be no greater reward for a hard day's work of gathering, boiling, grinding, and preparing a meal.

Right after dinner, Hosta gets up silently and begins walking back to the fields to spend the night with some of the other men and boys who will watch their fields all night long. Many of the younger boys don't like being out in the fields at all because witches are most active at night. The younger boys stay together and close to the small brush shelters that have been built close to the fields. They gather together and keep each other company, never letting on to anyone that they each felt a little fearful of who or what might be out in the shadows. They often build small fires for both light and a little warmth during this early part of the summer season. Sometimes off in the distance, a coyote howls or an owl is heard. The boys throw more wood on their fires and smear some ashes on their foreheads because they were taught it will help keep the witches away.

"Hi, Tokie." Hosta says to his younger brother who has also come out to join some of the younger boys this night.

"Hi brother," young Tokie responded. "I came to help you tonight."

Hosta smiles to himself because he knows the bright moon is the real reason his younger brother came out into the fields tonight. Hosta had done the same thing years before feeling that being in these fields under a full moon was somehow more tolerable than when it was dark and uninviting. The worst times, of course, were the nights before the harvest in fall when it would not only be dark but bitterly cold as well. And if a late season rain came, it could be doubly miserable and the witches would have enjoyed this misery.

Last fall Hosta had become very ill within a few days of having spent a cold and miserable night out in these very fields. Had it not been for his Hosta's uncle bringing in a witch doctor soon after his becoming ill, he might not have lived through the harvest last season. Life is quite precarious, and Hosta knows very well that you must watch out for yourself at all times.

Hosta's uncle is named Tye and he is Say's younger brother. He is a strong, well-built man about three years younger than his sister. He has short, dark hair, and dark, deep-set eyes. Like Hosta, Tye is quite tall and stands nearly six feet in height. He is a quiet and intelligent man who continues to earn the respect of the people in his clan. He is an excellent farmer and among his many skills and abilities, Tye is a gifted hunter with excellent marksmanship. Because of his interest in hunting, he is learning to become a Hunt Chief which is an important and well-respected ceremonial position in his community.

Just two seasons ago, Tye participated in a marriage ceremony and now has a wife. Together they have a beautiful daughter who is just learning how to walk. A son was stillborn last spring and it is believed that the witches took this child. Tye has already consulted with one of the village's medicine men to see what can be done to prevent another of his children from being unborn.

In addition to being Hosta's uncle, Tye is also the young man's ceremonial father. He was selected for this important position when Hosta was born and he will be responsible for all the religious training and education of his nephew. Children are raised in a way that allows them to imitate their parents' behavior and young boys are taught to observe and copy their fathers. Hosta recalls tumbling from his blankets just after sunrise when he would hear his father rise. He would watch him say morning prayers and take a pinch of corn meal and toss it in the air as an offering to the gods of the dawn.

Hosta would follow his father to the fields as soon as he was old enough, and he would always look forward to accompanying him on hunting trips. Hosta's father was an excellent craftsman who made bows, flint knives, bone awls, and was also one of the better "knappers," who made excellent arrowheads. Hosta caught on quickly and closely watched and imitated these necessary skills.

Just as important to the education of all young men is religious training, and Hosta's Uncle Tye will spend a great deal of time providing him with all relevant and important information. It was five seasons ago that Hosta began the process of being initiated into his mother's and uncle's society. He was first taught the more important legends of his people. The various rituals along with the first of many chants were taught so Hosta could begin to participate in the important ceremonies of his clan. If he had been interested, Hosta could have worked hard and asked to be considered for training as a medicine man. This would have required him to do little else for several years than sit at the feet of his elders to learn the additional chants, ceremonies, and mysterious ways of the healing men. But that was not to Hosta's liking, although he did spend a great deal of time learning many of the important things that manhood and the ways of his clan would require of him in the years to come.

Most of this final initiation and training took place last fall and winter in the large kiva that was near Tye's village. Throughout this time everyone participated in a number of day-long ceremonies led by chanting priests as well as all of the newly initiated members. It is through these lengthy songs and chants that the history and legends of his people were told, retold, and embellished. His people have no written record of their lives or their history, but what important things are known have been repeated in song and verse over hundreds of years. These nearly endless songs may go on throughout the night, but as late fall and winter are more quiet and a relaxing time for the people, and these activities are enjoyed by young and old men alike.

The kiva is the central meeting place for the men and not only serves as the main ceremonial center but also as a club room, workshop, and also as a dormitory for many in Hosta's society. Most unmarried, divorced, or separated men sleep here if their mother's house is too crowded with younger children or grandparents. Husbands who don't particularly care to spend great amounts of time with their in-laws also make great use of the kiva which often acts as an important sanctuary from the arguments and conflicts common to all people who live in close proximity with their relatives.

The training and education of young people is handled in other important ways as well. Hosta and his uncle spend many long hours in private discussions together as Tye explains the legends and beliefs of his tribe and clan. Important ceremonial information is passed down through stories which are repeated over and over. Tye will continue to be nephews' primary confidant and will teach him all of the ways of his clan and village. It is a task that Tye takes very seriously.

In this society, a child is always born into its mother's clan, and never into the father's. The matrilineal nature of society means that when a man and woman marry, the man is never allowed to become a full member of his wife's clan. He will remain a part of his own clan throughout life and any children produced in the marriage will become members of the mother's clan. Property also belongs to the women. Any inheritance of goods or property remains outside the husband's reach. Although the husband lives with his wife in her house, he often spends more time with his own clan than with the one into which he has married.

Marriage is not allowed to take place between two members of the same clan because members of the same clan are considered to be brothers and sisters. There is a strictly enforced taboo against intermarriage. In addition, it is generally impossible for a young man to select his future mate. It is the primary responsibility of the elders of his clan to arrange for a pairing and selection of a suitable mate. This is far too important of a task to be left to a young man aged seventeen or eighteen. And it was in knowing of this great truth that Hosta had spent so much time fretting to himself.

It was Tye whom Hosta had come out this evening to find. It would not be a difficult task, because most of the men from the various villages will be out in the fields this moonlit evening. No ceremonies were planned for the immediate future and so many of the men have come to the fields to light fires and sit nearby to engage in conversation and perhaps do a little gambling as well. Gambling is an important pastime and a common indulgence among the men, as much of the exchange of necessary goods is done through gambling as it is by trading. Sometimes the stakes are high and a fine piece of jewelry may be the prize. More commonly, however, insignificant or fairly common items are in play.

The contest itself may be a simple guessing contest or some minor game of skill. Mostly, gambling is a pure game of chance, and that is what most interests the men who play. In a typical game of chance, a common object like a small carved bone is thrown on the floor with the winner being decided by the manner in which the bones turn up.

A number of these minor games of chance are going on in the fields as Hosta walks north toward one of the fires. He immediately recognizes Tye who is laughing at something or another with one of the men who is about to become involved in the next game.

"Hosta, it's good to see you," Tye sings out upon seeing him approach.

"Hello, Uncle," Hosta replies as the two of them smile at one another and begin to walk slowly away from the others.

Tye puts his arm around the back of his nephew and asks about the well-being of his sister.

"She is fine and we are doing well," is Hosta's reply.

"Still no word about your father I hear," Tye remarks. "But until we have word otherwise, we will continue asking about him and he might yet return to us."

Hosta looks into his uncle's eyes trying to smile and give Tye reassurance that no one, not even a son, has yet given up on seeing the safe return of his father.

Tye grabs Hosta closer to him and gives his hair a good rubbing.

The two continue walking towards the fields where several of the younger boys was running and yelling at one another seeming to have a good time playing some kind of chase game.

"Be careful out there," Tye calls out to the boys. Upon seeing the likes of an adult nearby the boys run off leaving Hosta and Tye virtually alone in the fields.

His heart pounded a bit harder and he felt a bit of anxiety as he was concerned about how to initiate a conversation, Hosta turns to Tye and says, "Uncle, I must tell you something."

"Tell me something? What is that?"

The anxiety seems to melt away inside Hosta now that he has initiated this important conversation. After all, he had rehearsed what he was about to say more than a few times over the last month or so. Hosta sits down on the edge of the planted field and Tye joins him, sitting directly in front of his nephew. What could possibly be of concern to this fine young man?

"Uncle, I am told that I keep our fields well planted and that our harvests have been very good. Father has shown me how to make good arrows and the fine bow he gave me has brought home many deer and rabbits. We have stored much grain and have never been without the good things provided by our Mother Earth."

Tye listens intently to his nephew and looks directly into his eyes. For the very first time Tye begins to think quite differently about this young man. Such a conversation has never before taken place between them although they certainly have previously spoken about many important matters. This is different. This conversation has been initiated by Hosta, and Tye's eyes show great respect.

"At the planting ceremony last month, I again saw the young lady who is known to her family as Katti. I remember seeing her before at some of the earlier planting ceremonies, but I did not feel anything toward her. She is very beautiful. I believe that I am in love with her and I would like to know if it would be possible for you to help me in asking that she and I marry."

There. It was out and in the open. Hosta takes a deep breath and looks for his uncle's reaction.

A wide smile emerges on Tye's face. "Hosta, I am happy to hear what you have told me." Tye reaches out both his arms and rests his hands on Hosta's shoulders. "I know of the young lady you mention. I know her people are from the Water Clan. Yes, she is a beautiful girl and you have a good eye and good heart. The two of you would make an excellent family and I will do everything in my power to help you, but you know what must be done."

Hosta sits up straight and is most satisfied that his uncle seems not only to understand but suggests assistance in the matter as well. He could not be more pleased and is glad to have this matter now in the open.

"Yes, I know what must be done, Uncle Tye, and I am most pleased to hear that you will help me."

What was not spoken about were the very real problems this situation would cause to everyone involved. This is not generally how things are done. Marriage is an important event and the union of strong and healthy young men and women is a responsibility that all members of a clan cannot afford to take lightly. There are stories of other young people who took it upon themselves to attempt marriage without the benefit of family participation or acceptance. These situations most often resulted in either very bitter feelings, broken hearts, and the man would often succumb to a reverence for his elders and take the responsibility for terminating any further contact between himself and the woman.

"In two days time, right after the sun rises we will go together to your mother and talk of this matter," Tye says. "I will come to your house early; so wait for me."

A coyote howls somewhere in the distance and breaks their conversation for just an instant. Moonlight blue shadows spread along the ground as Tye and Hosta slowly rise from their place near the field and walk towards the snapping fires and the warmth and comfort that only a combination of friendship and kinship can provide.

Just after returning to his own home later that evening, Tye helps to make sure the baby is comfortably asleep. His wife Myria thinks it is most unusual for Tye to return home so early, and it is. He goes over to sit in front of his wife and sleeping child.

"My nephew believes it is time for him to take a wife," Tye whispers quietly to his wife.

She quickly looks up at him and asks, "Do you think that is such a good idea? His father has not returned and there is much concern in the family already. There is no time now for them to help select a suitable girl."

Tye faces Myria and rocks back and forth, not knowing quite how to break the rest of the news to her. But he is a direct and straightforward man and there is no real reason to hold out.

"Hosta already knows the woman he wants to marry."

"What?" Myria asks with surprise and a smile on her face. "Is he seeing someone now?"

"Not exactly, but you know that Hosta is a young man who knows his own mind and I'm certain he believes in what he wants to do."

The conversation continues for a time and Myria soon discovers who the young lady is and reveals that she knows Katti's mother and even remembers spending some time a few years ago working with Katti on one of the summer ceremonial events. She appears delighted with the choice and even welcomes the opportunity of getting to know her better. But the information is far too important to be kept secret. Myria convinces her husband that someone should approach the young lady's family quickly to determine what difficulties might lie ahead of these two fine young people. Myria would enjoy being the one to speak with young Katti, but that would not be proper. Tye agrees to find a reason to visit her village within the next day or two to see if he can arrange an initial contact and discussion.

All matters involving human interaction, including love and hate, are of particular interest to Tye. He is quite skilled in many things including matters of compassion and understanding. Like his own father, he is often called upon by others in nearby villages to help in resolving disputes or negotiating solutions to various problems. It has even been suggested at one time that Tye might make a good chief because of his excellent skills in resolving problems. Although never spoken about much, it is certainly true that one of the most important characteristics of a chief is the ability to heal the wounds of bruised egos and find ways to settle disputes and contentious matters as diplomatically and yet forcefully as possible.

Late in the afternoon of the following day, after all of his chores are completed and after having some time to compose his thoughts, Tye walks to Katti's village and spends a couple of hours visiting. The conversations go well and Tye is asked to have dinner with Katti, her mother, and younger sister.

On the way back to his own family later that evening, Tye considers whether or not he should talk with his nephew about the meeting with Katti. After giving thought to every aspect of things, he decides it would be best not to say anything to anyone else just yet. He will let things take their own normal course but feels strongly that if it looks like a serious setback might occur, he will not hesitate to play a larger role in whatever negotiations or further discussions might be needed.

CHAPTER *four*

A bright morning sun quickly warmed a slight chill in the air. It was going to be another warm summer day; yet it would not be so hot to impede progress in the work day ahead.

Jerry, Kay, and Kelly had once again arrived at the project site well before Diane and I were able to get ourselves together. Kay was busy unloading our trenching tools and Kelly had staked out a new one-by-ten-meter section just south of the kiva site. This area had been identified in the initial archaeological summary as possibly containing a series of room blocks and she was going to begin excavating a section to verify what might lie below. The location of room blocks here would be fairly typical of this particular region. Prior archaeological research projects have shown that this area was occupied over hundreds of years and had seen a wide variety of habitation types. The area Kelly had just staked out was generally south of our kiva, and just south of the room block a fairly large midden had been identified. The scatter pattern of surface materials and other features was typical of archaeological sites in the region that had been excavated over the past fifty years or so.

Jerry was setting up his electronic surveying equipment in anticipation of taking a number of identifying notations as our work progressed through the day.

"Sleep well?" Jerry asked as he saw Diane and me walking up to the site.

"Well, kinda, but I kept hitting my head on the top of the motor home every time I turned over," Diane responded with a chuckle.

Last night we decided neither the over-cab bunk nor the two bunks in the back of our motor home were going to be comfortable with both of us occupying them. So we split up. I took the over-cab bunk and Diane landed in the top bunk in back. It was not the most ideal of arrangements we've ever endured, but we could cope with it for the week.

"Well, you guys can get to work whenever you want," Jerry said. "I think we'll just keep working on the kiva and go on down another ten centimeters from north to south. We're probably down far enough that we should begin to encounter some artifacts, so take it easy and we'll screen everything we haul out."

We eagerly dug in and started the routine of scraping down layers of dirt. At this level, which was about a foot or so down from the surface, we ran into a number of rather large roots of the nearby trees that had easily penetrated the kiva area. Luckily, Jerry had a couple of branch cutters in his tool box and the network of smaller roots was easily dispensed with. A few roots were an inch or two in diameter and required a saw to remove them.

An archaeological dig involves several routine procedures but never produces the same results day after day. Although the anticipation of occasionally finding things is always present, and there are always new and interesting things that might show up while you're breaking up the soil, satisfying finds are never assured. A few rocks began appearing which may or may not be associated with a more orderly stacking of rocks that might indicate someone actually placed the rocks on purpose. On the other hand, they just might have slipped down from the surface at some previous time and randomly appear. There was always a variety of interesting things to be discovered and interpreted, but the digging process itself was nearly always the same. Loosened dirt needed to be scooped up, hauled out of the excavation, and carried down a small hill to be shoveled or dumped into the screen that would then be shaken and the material thoroughly examined.

Our routine continued for an hour or so and Diane was finding a number of pottery fragments. Some were of the corrugated type; others had dark hand-painted decoration on a gray body. None of the pottery sherds was more than a couple of inches in size, and no evidence of fully intact earthenware was yet discovered. A few flakes of flint material were also appearing, but nothing unusual or terribly interesting.

Just before taking our midmorning break, Edmund's pickup appeared. We saw the driver's side door open slowly and saw him making his way cautiously up to the site. From a distance it looked like his left hand was wrapped with a white cloth of some kind. We didn't pay much attention to this and Jerry went over to greet Edmund who seemed to be walking a little slower than normal.

Kay sat on the edge of the kiva writing up details of the morning's activity. She and Kelly exchanged information on the routine of their lives and occasionally remarked on the progress of our project. It was a pleasant and relaxing time and the day itself could not have been better. The temperature was climbing into the mid 80s, and a light breeze continued to provide assurance that the day would not become too warm and uncomfortable.

We all took a break around ten and watched Edmund's pickup making its way back to the road. Jerry was waving goodbye, and walked over to our spot in the shade.

"Edmund really hurt himself yesterday," Jerry reported to us as he came to share a cold drink.

"What happened?" Kelly asked.

"Did you see the bandages wrapped around his left hand?" Jerry asked. "He really mangled his hand at the quarry yesterday afternoon."

Jerry told us the story. Some time after visiting our site yesterday and showing Jerry the stone ax he had found, Edmund joined his crew and went back to the rock quarry to continue working on some project or another. He and another crew member were moving a bunch of rock and somehow his left hand got crushed between a couple of good-sized rocks. Three fingers of his left hand were badly hurt. The skin was torn and bones, tendons, and nerves were affected. One of the crew had to drive Edmund into town and at the local hospital an afternoon of medical attention was given to his fingers and hand. They gave him some pain killers, and then completely wrapped his left hand in a solid mass of bandages and put the whole thing into a cast. It didn't look like Edmund had a very pleasant afternoon.

"Could result in some permanent damage," Jerry indicated, "which is pretty bad for a guy who depends on manual labor for his livelihood."

"That's awful," Kelly responded, "but he's still able to drive I see."

We all chuckled knowing that a mangled left hand wasn't about to deter Edmund from driving his own pickup truck although you could easily tell the guy was in some discomfort from the way he moved.

The next several hours of the morning were spent in the routine we seemed to have established. Because of the leisurely pace of our digging, Jerry and I engaged in a conversation about the history of this area, and I asked him to help explain and interpret some of what I had been reading recently. I was particularly curious about his thoughts concerning what we were excavating, the people who might have lived here, and what artifacts we were likely to find as we continued.

I had read that this area of Colorado has been inhabited by man for at least 12,000 years. Many scientists believe that man has been here much longer, although we may never know the entire story. What we do seem to know today in piecing together a variety of evidence from various sources is this:

About 37,000 years ago nearly a sixth of the entire world's surface area was covered by massive glaciers, some of the ice being nearly a mile thick. The formation of these ice sheets required megatons of condensed water to be sucked from the world's oceans, which caused them to recede so greatly that in some places the level of the seas were lowered as much as 300 feet or more. One of the areas where this happened was between northeastern Siberia and northwestern Alaska. During this time, known as the Pleistocene Epoch—or more commonly referred to as the Ice Age—a 56-mile strip of the ocean's floor was exposed at the Bering Straits which allowed grazing animals and other exotic life an opportunity to cross from the Asian continent into North America using the exposed "land bridge."

The earliest human inhabitants of North America are thought to be associated with ancient migratory hunters who arrived here from Asia by way of this land bridge. Precisely when these people first arrived is still uncertain and may remain one of those questions that may never be answered fully. Respected scholars offer us a wide range of opinions and we may never know when the first humans set foot on the soil of this New World. But it is almost certain that the migration was not a singular event and occurred over several thousands of years.

Because no one can provide absolute and unchallenged evidence about when man first appeared in North America, there have been several reasonable schools of thought concerning when man first inhabited our continent. Some respected archaeologists offer radio carbon dates for human habitation sites along with very crude lithic materials that date back some 20,000 years before the present. Interestingly, most of the evidence used to support the theories concerning the earliest arrival of man come from irregular stone flakes which have the appearance of being trimmed at their edges. These materials were not found in Alaska, Canada, or the United States, but in Mesoamerica and South America. There is even some archaeological evidence that supports a theory that trans-Pacific migrations may have taken place to the Americas, although there is no definitive proof of this, and it is nearly certain that such migrations would not have taken place prior to 3,000 years before the present. It has also been suggested that man could have migrated from east to west across the North Atlantic at some point. A number of interesting and reasonable theories have been advanced concerning how and when man first set foot on American soil.

Ancient artifacts and fire sites have been discovered in some concentrations among the limestone plateaus of the current State of Texas where some of the oldest known evidence of man in the New World has been identified. Archaeologists and other scientists have discovered that these Ice Age people possessed massive teeth and had longer heads than any race of modern man. Their skeletal structure is quite unlike that of the people who would later be known as the prehistoric American Indians. The families of man are all "Homo Sapiens" although it is now believed there is a true distinction between the very first American "Big Game Hunters" who inhabited North America and the later "Paleo-Indian" people.

Both of these very early people led entirely nomadic lives for several thousands of years. And then they seemed to vanish and there is about a five-hundred-year gap in our archaeological record. It isn't clear if the first Big Game Hunters of the Southwest simply moved on to places like the Great Plains or to other areas, or if, in fact, the people were replaced by an entirely new group of Asian migrants. We don't know if these people simply died out or if they changed in such significant ways that we can no longer recognize them. It might be that the next group of inhabitants were descendants of the Big Game Hunters or they might even be new arrivals to the Southwest perhaps migrating north into the region from Mesoamerica, or again over the still-existing land bridge. There is some evidence to support a number of claims and perhaps all hypotheses are correct to some extent.

The tracking of early man in North America is a fascinating and intriguing mystery, but contemporary science is narrowing the gap in our knowledge. Geneticists have been able to analyze human DNA which strongly supports an Asian homeland connection for nearly all Native American people. This commonly shared genetic past dates these populations to between 15 and 30,000 years before the present. Respected DNA experts have hypothesized that more than 95 percent of all Native America people are descendants of a single founder population which crossed that ancient land bridge during the late Ice Age.

These newer Asian nomadic people ultimately migrated into southwestern Colorado and there appears to be enough evidence to support a belief that these people were here at least 12,500 years ago. These people possessed fire, wore heavy clothing made of skin and furs, and used tools made of flint and bone. They were simple hunters who followed herds of game and appear to have been quite unconcerned about where they were.

The hunting of animals was a critical activity shared by both men and women. Men would ambush the animals, usually around a watering hole or similar gathering place. These early hunters fashioned spearheads made of stone which had detachable shafts. The use of a detachable shaft is indicative of the sophistication of these early hunters who obviously learned that a wounded animal could work out an embedded point if the shaft remained intact. A detachable spear point was used to hasten death of their prey. Once the animals were dead, the women would use sharp stone knives to strip hide from the animals and remove fat, flesh, and meat for use as food and the valuable hides for clothing and other needs.

Over several thousand years of human occupation throughout North America, the earth's climate changed gradually. Things got warmer, the polar ice caps started to melt, and the ocean waters started to rise. With that, the entire geography of the southwestern United States began to change dramatically. The Bering land bridge slowly receded, but before it disappeared, the horse and camel that developed in America migrated into Asia. Bison and mammoth reversed directions and crossed into America from Asia. At some point the land bridge disappeared below the rising seas and forever entrapped both man and game on this side of the continent. At the same time the area became much drier and annual mean temperatures rose about three or four degrees. Annual rainfall in the area decreased three to four inches and the lush vegetation on which larger mammals depended for their survival became scarce. So did these magnificent animals. Ultimately the camels, elephants, mastodons, prehistoric horses, and other large species became extinct in North America. Scientists have suggested that the very first Big Game Hunters may have become extinct as well.

In the 1920s a New Mexican cowboy by the name of George McJunkin found a number of large animal remains at a place called Wild Horse Gulch which is about eight miles west of Folsom, New Mexico. Reports of this find spread quickly among interested scientists, and paleontologists from the Colorado Museum of Natural History in Denver excavated these ancient bison bones that were buried beneath several layers of clay and gravel. The scientists were shocked when they found two pieces of chipped flint which were simply lying loose in the dirt close by. The chips were clearly artifacts of human manufacture and later an even more exciting discovery was nearby. Another flint "point", still in its original position, was found embedded in the clay that surrounded a bison's rib.

In addition, the scientists discovered at least nineteen beautifully hand-crafted projectile points that had been made from obsidian, rhyolite, jasper and other minerals that are commonly referred to today as "Folsom points." This particular site and its remains have been dated to around 10,000 to 11,000 years before the present.

After the Folsom discoveries there was universal acceptance of man's presence in the American Southwest since at least the late Pleistocene Era. These discoveries changed the rules and archaeologists continued verifying their conclusions which led to even more exciting discoveries.

In 1932, about 150 miles south of Folsom, a road crew digging in a gravel pit near a place called Blackwater Draw, dug up a large stone tool along with a huge animal tooth. Someone was alert enough to contact scientists who responded quickly to the discovery which is near the town of Clovis, New Mexico. Archaeologists from the Academy of Natural Sciences of Philadelphia and the University of Pennsylvania Museum mounted a full expedition to Blackwater Draw and in 1933 found additional stone tools similar to those found at Folsom.

A great breakthrough came first in 1936 and again the next year when archaeologists dug below the Folsom finds and located similar but distinctively different spear points associated with remains of mammoths which we also refer to as the American elephant. These very earliest of man-made lithic tools are called Clovis Points, and date to about 11,500 to 10,500 years before the present.

In the 1950s, University of Arizona archaeologists discovered two other kill sites which have also been dated to about 11,000 years ago. One of the Arizona kill sites includes the remains of an extinct mammoth where eight stone spearheads were discovered among the skeletal remains of the 13-foot tall animal. The second site includes the bones of nine elephants along with a primitive horse and a bison. Nearby, a fire pit was located and ashes from it were radiocarbon dated to about 9,000 B.C., again verifying the probable date of this early human activity. It is likely the fire pit may have been used to roast meat from the nearby animal kill.

The discovery and dating of the Folsom points was an important event in the difficult task of tracking early man in North America. To this day, the actual discovery of Folsom man himself has eluded archaeologists. In 1947 scientists were working on a dig site in a dry lake bed near Mexico City after hearing reports that natives in the area had located a number of mammoth bones. In the same layer, and near where some of the mammoth bones were found, the partial skeleton of a man was unearthed. There remains some skepticism about the true age of these bones, known as Tepexpan Man, but the layer in which the human remains was discovered shows evidence of materials that have been dated to about 15,000 years of age.

In 1952, and about a mile from the first discovery, another mammoth skeleton was found in which six finely-made stone implements were also located. One of these was either a spear or dart point that lodged between two ribs of the mammoth, providing further support to the belief that this animal had been tracked and killed by man. More important, the skeleton of another human was located nearby, adding to the credible evidence of man's 15,000 year coexistence with the big game of North America. Science has yet to discover, and may never find, a complete or intact human skeleton that dates earlier than 15,000 years on this side of the world's great oceans.

As the big game disappeared, people's diets also began to change. There were other smaller animal species including deer and big-horn sheep that inhabited the region so needed nutritional protein was readily available. In addition to being hunters, the people also became gatherers of a wide variety of edible plants. Nuts, berries, roots, and seeds were plentiful throughout North America. Much smaller game like rabbits, rodents, birds, and squirrels could be hunted with spears and dart throwers known as *atlatls*. Even sophisticated snares were developed for hunting small game and diets became varied as the people became more proficient in their use of resources. The people also developed utensils like grinding stones to help process the wild seeds they were collecting.

Trays and baskets were also developed to assist in the collection and preparation of food. Resins and natural gums were used to help waterproof storage containers that were usually made of natural fibers or were shaped out of gourds. Over time, cooking techniques and dietary habits changed radically which led to one of the greatest human evolution's of all times—the shift away from a largely nomadic way of life to one where agriculture, the planting and cultivation of plants, became the primary way of life of these early people.

This dramatic change occurred about 5,000 or 6,000 years ago and began with a combination of semi-permanent and semi-nomadic lifestyles. Crops were planted in cultivated fields but the people still spent a considerable amount of time away from their fields while hunting game. The success of limited agriculture was entirely dependent on both the amount and timing of natural rainfall. In some years crops would grow abundantly but in others, crops failed to mature because of widely varying climatic conditions. This feast or famine pattern existed for a long period and did not end until storage systems and more dependable agricultural practices developed.

It was not until water resource management and control techniques appeared around 500 B.C. that there was an increased reliance on the growing of crops that ultimately led to a radical change in the state and condition of human life. Around the time of Christ's birth halfway around the world, there was only a handful of permanent living sites, or villages, in the American Southwest. Most tribes of people were still semi-nomadic, who established only modest base camps near their fields, and spent the bulk of their time hunting and gathering over a wide area.

It has also been determined that various locations in the Four Corners area were inhabited for a few hundred years at a time and then abandoned for a few hundred years before people came back to resettle the area. It is not uncommon to find earlier sites buried under the remains of more contemporary sites. Throughout the world, civilizations tend to built newer structures above or on the remains of previous towns and villages. Just as some animals seem to retrace the steps of their ancestors, so too does man seem to migrate from and back to previously occupied sites.

As mentioned before, it was also the development of more permanent dwelling structures that assisted in the introduction of more stable living conditions for these early Americans. We today know some of these people as the Anasazi, and it is their past we are sifting through and attempting to more fully discover and interpret.

Over a 2,500 to 3,000 year period, these early agriculturists made greater and more sophisticated use of their resources, actually stored grains for future use, managed to control and alter water resources, and built elaborate roadway and ceremonial centers over several hundreds of miles of the San Juan River Basin. Although certainly not the most remarkable or advanced people of our prehistory, they nevertheless comprise an intriguing component of our American heritage.

And then, about seven hundred years ago, they all disappeared. Almost everyone left. Elaborate and sophisticated villages and cliff dwellings were abandoned. Some of their habitation structures were ritually burned as the people left. Some locations were abandoned virtually overnight and some people seemed to linger for a few more years and then quietly left.

For most of the past hundred years or so, archaeologists and ethnologists have suggested that the primary reason for this abandonment was largely related to several environmental changes—primarily radical climatic change. There is ample evidence from tree-ring dating that shows a twenty-four year period of severe drought in the region that peaked around 1276 and again in 1299 A.D. Some years were moderately dry while others showed clear evidence of severely dry periods. It is likely that several dry years produced tragically poor harvests of essential foods. Crops suffered but so did wild food plants which forced larger game to seek food and water elsewhere. Even smaller game was affected by the multiple years of drought.

The priests must have been completely mystified about the reasons their chants and ceremonies were not working. Were the gods angry or inattentive, or were the priests slowly losing their powers over the important aspects of life itself? In many of the villages death and disease were decreasing the populations and the medicine men seemed to be growing powerless. Tragic stories told of some villagers who had to sacrifice their precious seed corn supplies to prevent starvation. Other stories told of a group of villagers who raided a neighboring village to steal what little food might be found. People fought and killed one another and some reports suggested that human flesh had been boiled and eaten by some of the starving people. It was certainly a very trying time for these prehistoric ancestors.

Recent archaeological interpretation of the data, however, suggests that the people could have been satisfactorily adaptive to the so-called Great Drought. By this time artificial reservoirs were built to collect and store water for domestic and agricultural use. A wide system of elaborate check-dams were built across ravines and along hillsides that provided terraces where eroding topsoil's were captured. These terraces not only provided for additional tillable acreage but also helped to trap and store runoff water.

Sophisticated dams were built in natural drainage channels just above canyon pour-offs that trapped rainwater runoff and helped feed it into underlying bedrock from which it would emerge in springs. In addition, larger and larger pottery jars were being made and a variety of harvested grains, seeds, and plant materials of all kinds were stored in above and below ground rooms. Sophisticated computer-generated population estimates make it difficult for most scientists to envision a broad scale and rapid retreat simply because of these climate changes, and make it hard to accept earlier held beliefs that food supplies simply ran out. This leaves a single and perhaps more probable reason for the gradual abandonment. This theory suggests that people simply migrated out of the area for purely social, political, and religious reasons.

It is unlikely we will ever know the complete story or all of the specific reasons for the abandonment because prehistory is just that. However, it is false to assume that these people simply disappeared from the face of the earth. They did not. They migrated generally south into New Mexico and Arizona. Today, you can shake the hand of an Anasazi ancestor as easily as you can shake the hand of any other neighbor. And we can't believe for a minute that the cultural heritage of the Anasazi has in any way completely disappeared. All we need to do is look at many of the fine crafts we can easily find throughout the Southwest. Listen to the stories you may hear being told, or attend one of the sacred ceremonial dances of the Hopi, Zuni, or other Pueblo peoples if you are ever invited. Yesterday is alive and well in the Four Corners area.

Right after lunch, we found something.

Just between the bench and the outer wall of the kiva, about a foot down, a light tan and circular piece of pottery became exposed. I was working in this area, not with the standard trowel—which I don't care for very much—but with a small patiche. This handy tool is more commonly used by geologists as it has a double-sided metal head which is attached to a hammer-like wooden handle. One end of the metal head has a flat sided piece; the other a narrowing pick-like end. You can move a lot of dirt with this tool, but it is not always as delicate as a trowel for the kind of work we were currently engaged in. But I liked the tool anyway and tried to be as cautious with it as I could. Luckily, Jerry was watching me carefully as I began working right after lunch, and he has pretty good eyes and cautioned me to slow down a bit before digging more aggressively.

"What's this?" I asked somewhat excitedly.

Diane was also working close by and she stopped to come over and ask, "What did you find?"

"Could be just another sherd," Jerry said, "but then again it could be the rim of a cup or bowl."

"Take it easy, Greenlee," Diane implored, "don't chop it to pieces."

I gave her a "not-to-worry-I'll-take-care-of-it" glance but did slow up quite a bit and scraped away some of the dirt around the side of the rim. Slowly, ever so slowly, the object began to emerge from the earth. As I took away more and more of the dirt around this object, another similar rim slightly left and about three inches away also appeared.

"Looks like another rim," I said to no one in particular. And I began picking away at both of these objects until the first one I was working on started to reveal itself. The circumference of the rim was about three inches or so, and it was taking on a shape. Hopefully, it was not just a piece of something but, in fact, intact.

"It looks like a cup, or the bowl of a ladle," Jerry said, "so be careful and if it is a ladle, check to see if a handle is still fully attached. You don't wanna chop it off."

I went a little slower yet, scratching now with my fingers alone trying to loosen the dirt in all directions around the thing. After about five minutes or so, the object started to come loose from the surrounding dirt. By this time the entire crew had come over to see what was going on. Kelly and Kay sat on the rim of the kiva while I dug a bit deeper and slowly turned the rounded object in a clockwise–

counter clockwise direction. With that, it came loose. No handle seemed to be attached. But there it was, a perfectly intact bowl of an ancient pottery ladle. The bowl was filled with compacted dirt and as I put the thing in my hand and showed it all around, I finally knew what all of this hard labor was all about. I had found something. Nothing great. Nothing that would require a rewriting of the archaeological history of the Southwest, but there it was. Something.

"Let's clean it up," Kay said.

"Neat," Diane said cheerily.

"Great," said I, "let's see what else we've got next to it."

After a bit more picking and dirt removal, another and slightly smaller rim and bowl was becoming apparent. I made sure the work went slowly just in case a handle might be attached to this piece, but unfortunately none was found.

Within a few more minutes, this ladle bowl also came loose. It was equally well preserved and you could see where at one time a handle had been attached to both of the items. By the time this piece was unearthed, Kay had removed the remaining dirt from inside the first ladle. She spit directly in the bowl and moved her index finger round and round on the inside where a distinctive black decoration became evident on the gray clay body. The second cup bowl was also being worked on for dirt removal, and it too had a nicely painted design in the bowl although it was a bit less interesting than the first one.

"Nice going," Kay said, "we'll take some shots with the transit and get a record for when we write up the report."

The momentary excitement now over, we went on with the project a bit more enthusiastically than before now having found something a bit more interesting than the many pieces of things we had been finding so far.

Digging near where the ladles had been found, large fragments of a corrugated pottery bowl or jug were also located. It might have been that the two ladles were placed inside the larger corrugated jug at some time, and set on the bench of the kiva for some reason. Perhaps it was part of a prehistoric ceremony. Perhaps it was nothing more than leaving a rather common and utilitarian object behind for some unknown reason.

We then took a brief mid-afternoon break, although Diane seemed determined once again to keep on working, and her persistence paid off. While scraping away at the next layer down, she came across a small piece of bone. It was not immediately possible to determine if the bone was from some animal, or if it was human.

Later, in one of the loads of material I took over to screen, another unusual object surfaced. I carried it back with a couple of pottery sherds and asked Kay what it might be.

"Looks like a tooth," she reported, "maybe a molar. Take a look, Kelly."

Kelly climbed out of her deepening excavation and came over to take a look. "Yep, that's what it is all right, I think we might have found somebody."

"Well, I think I just found more of it," Diane reported from inside the hole.

We all went over to take a look at what she was handing up to us. A quick inspection by everyone later confirmed it was the bone of a human finger. Within a few minutes, Diane found a circular bone and after it was shown around it was confirmed to be a vertebra. Whatever, or whoever, it looked like we were excavating a possible burial. With that information, Jerry indicated he needed to make contact with the local Sheriff's Department and perhaps even the local Coroner as well. Jerry walked over, looked at the materials, took some notes, and went off to use his cellular phone and contact whatever local authorities needed to be notified.

I thought the whole business of needing to contact the Sheriff and Coroner was a bit of overkill, but I really didn't know much about the whole process either. It was later explained to me that most of the time local authorities would simply inquire about how far down the remains were found. It they had not been located at or near the surface, little follow-up was necessary. Had the remains been found closer to the surface, they might indicate a rather recent deposit of a body which might require further investigation. I guess the more I thought about it, the more sense the whole thing made.

"Think it's a boy or girl?" Diane asked as she continued scraping away in the area where many of the bones were being unearthed.

"Don't know," was the reply from Kay who carried with her a reference book illustrating the size, shape, and position of bones on the human skeleton and anatomy. She had obviously used this book many times before and both Kay and Kelly appeared to be quite familiar with the specific human remains we were recovering. "Can't really tell unless we find the pelvis, or something else that will give us a better clue."

We elected to name this unknown person "Pat" after the "Saturday Night Live" television program that at times had a skit featuring a sexually ambivalent character.

The warm and comfortable afternoon went on pleasantly. All of us were getting quite filthy once again with sweat combining easily with the loose dirt and dust. The work consisted of digging, sifting, recording, and wandering conversation about a wide variety of contemporary, political, and regional archaeological issues. Just before getting ready to call it a day, another pickup truck came bouncing up to the area where we had all parked our cars.

"Who's that?" Kay asked.

"Uh oh," Jerry said, "It's Edmund's pickup and Cecil's driving him. Don't say anything about Pat or neither one of 'em will ever come back."

Jerry went out to greet the two men. After standing around the pickup for a few minutes, all three of them got in and took off.

"Probably wants to show Jerry something," Kay said and we all went back to work.

Around 4:30 what little breeze had been blowing during the day managed to whip up a number of white billowy clouds to the west. Every now and then the sun would disappear under one of the growing cloud masses, and things would cool down comfortably. There were enough clouds building both to the west and down near Mesa Verde to suggest it might even rain before the day was over. That would have been welcome, as a light rain would help to keep the dust down, and we managed to make a lot of dust in the process.

"Well, I think it's about time to call it a day," Kelly suggested, and she got up from the spot where she was digging.

I hadn't paid too much attention to what she was doing all day long, so I invited myself over for a guided tour of her progress. The one-by-ten-meter space had been dug down about a foot or more at the northern end, and toward the south just shy of a foot. At that end, a mound of reddish clay appeared. Kelly explained that this reddish material was a rather thick collection of burned adobe. Along with this, she had discovered quite a bit of charcoal. In fact a number of the pieces were big enough that she wanted to stabilize the chunks and hope they were large enough for a lab to run a tree-ring analysis. She believed these large charcoal pieces were part of a roof support structure, and she had just begun working to remove one large beam. Rather than tackle that job today, she said it would be her first work priority the next day after talking things over with Jerry. It did seem quite evident that she had exposed the beginning of a series of surface rooms that might be storage, living, or work areas.

Just as we finished picking up all the tools and putting away the transit and were getting the kiva covered with a bit of plastic just in case it did rain during the night, Jerry came walking up the hill. Edmund's pickup truck was kicking up a bit of dust as it left the site and headed back to the road. There was some object in Jerry's right hand, and I couldn't quite make out what it was.

"What's happening?" I asked as Jerry walked toward us.

"Well," Jerry grinned, "its kinda interesting. You know Edmund told me about how he hurt his hand yesterday. I guess he talked things over with his uncle at lunch today and his uncle told him the reason he had this accident was really no accident at all."

We all looked intently at Jerry with puzzled looks on our faces.

"Seems the reason Edmund got his hand all messed up is because he found and handled that old stone ax he told us about yesterday. He left the damn thing in his pickup truck, and now because of what his uncle told him, he won't even get in let alone drive the truck unless someone removes it. So, he had Cecil drive him all the way over here to haul me back to where he's parked in order to get it."

Jerry held up his right hand. In it was a perfectly carved and chiseled ancient stone ax.

CHAPTER
five

Morning did not come quickly for Hosta. He had spent two rather restless nights sleeping in the fields. The nights weren't cold, or unpleasant, but he had difficulty relaxing and a deep sleep eluded him. Now with the sun just coming up, Hosta gets up and starts walking back to his home.

He passes one of the men of his village walking toward the fields, and they exchange a brief greeting. No one is awake when Hosta arrives home, although he can hear the faint sounds of people just beginning to rustle. To pass the time, Hosta rebuilds the fire from the previous night. It takes little effort to encourage the remaining coals to give new life to a handful of dried pine needles. Just as the fire is taking hold, Hosta looks up to see his uncle walking across the field. Hosta jumps up and runs out to greet Tye.

"Had any second thoughts about anything?" Tye asks Hosta as they walk along together.

"Oh, no, but I haven't slept very well, and I hope, I mean I sure want things to work out," Hosta replied as he took in a few deep breaths trying to relax.

They continue discussing the situation and it wasn't long before Say came around the corner and joined them.

She looked up in surprise and asked, "Why brother, what brings you here this fine morning? How did you know I could use your help today?"

"Good morning, sister. I didn't know there were any chores that you needed help with, but I'll be glad to do what I can," Tye replies.

He and his sister had always had an open and friendly relationship even when they were growing up together. They shared many hardships and many good times together. Now there was a slightly awkward pause before Tye looked at Hosta and then turned to his sister and said, "Actually, Hosta and I need to discuss an important matter with you which is why I've come."

Say quickly glances at her oldest son with a bit of concern and asks, "What is it that requires the two of you to talk with me? Have you received some word about Koya?"

Koya was always on everyone's mind. Right after planting their fields just about six weeks ago, nine men from the nearby villages left on one of their regular trading expeditions. Somehow members of the party got separated along the way. Six of the men returned together, and two others returned a few days later. But no one is certain where Koya might be, or whether he is still alive or had perhaps encountered some evil in his travels that might mean he would never return. Hosta felt a pang of guilt in talking with his mother about his own situation, knowing she certainly had been carrying the mental burden of a missing husband. But it was too late, he had opened the door and the matter needed to be discussed.

"No, we have not received any word about Koya," Tye replies, "but we must remain hopeful that he will return safely to us."

"Then what is it?" Say looks even more concerned.

"It is about a girl they call Katti," Hosta quickly responds to get the matter out in the open. His heart beats quickly and he could hardly contain any more anxiety. It was a relief to put the matter forward so it could be discussed.

Say listens intently as her oldest son and brother tells her everything of importance. She relaxes a bit as the conversation continues because in her heart, she knows that Hosta is completely ready to accept the responsibilities of marriage and starting his own family. He is an excellent hunter and farmer. Say taught him many things including the process of pottery-making for which she was well known throughout the region. Because he had grown up with a younger brother and sister, Hosta is familiar with the demands of child rearing and Say knows her oldest son will someday make an excellent father. But the thought of accepting this important change in all of their lives at this particular time was of concern and quite unsettling to her.

"We will call for a family council immediately to discuss this matter," Say replies as she reaches out her hand to touch the face of her son. "You are a man now, Hosta, and I respect your expression of affection for this young lady who is called Katti. If she is a worthy young woman, I do not believe the council will disallow your wish, but you know her family must also approve of this union. Do not let your heart know pain if this is not to be," she cautions.

"I believe each family will know of the strength of this marriage," Tye replies to his sister. "But your mother is correct, Hosta, there is still much that must be done in order for you to consider this union. You must not become impatient."

Hosta smiles, and is pleased with the initial reaction of his mother. He knows that what his uncle and mother are saying is true. If the elders of his family were not to approve of Katti, for whatever reason, they could immediately terminate any future contact between the two and any possibility of a marriage. He would have no ability to resist this decision, if it were made. At the same time, Katti's elders would undertake a similar process of decision-making. They would need to be assured that Hosta is a worthy young man who possesses necessary hunting and farming skills and is knowledgeable of the many important ceremonies that would become part of their future lives, and holds respect for the ways of their family's particular clan. Once each of the families has had adequate time to discuss all important matters, the two families would meet together and reach a formal agreement concerning the romance and its future. Katti's relatives would make demands of Hosta's family and would let it be known that certain gifts would be expected. In return, Katti would need to demonstrate her domestic abilities to Hosta's family. This would involve going to Say's home early some morning and for four days she would need to grind corn in front of Say and other female members of Hosta's family to prove that she was capable of performing this essential task. It would be backbreaking work, but if she wants to marry, her tasks must be done efficiently and productively. Hosta's family would then make a final decision concerning how well she performed this and other tasks that might be assigned to her. In the end, both families would either agree that the marriage can go forward, or they would render an unfavorable decision that means that Katti and Hosta would need to abandon their desire to be husband and wife.

Most of the actual work in having a marriage take place would rest on the shoulders of Katti's family. Their primary responsibility would be to build a house for the new couple to live in and will require a great amount of time to complete. The task must be performed around other important work like making sure that this season's crop is properly grown and harvested. An adequate food supply must be gathered and prepared during the summer and right after the harvest to ensure that a long and difficult winter will not leave anyone without adequate stores. At the earliest, all marriage preparations could not be completed much before the end of fall.

Hosta would also be kept quite busy if the marriage were to be agreed upon. It would be his responsibility to provide certain presents to his new wife. He could, for example, decide to make her a fine new pair of sandals, or he might want to weave her a soft and warm feather blanket. If he were to choose to be even more ambitious, he would hand-weave her a beautiful white cotton blanket.

All of these things seemed somewhat overpowering to Hosta at the moment, and nothing could yet be taken for granted. The first of many hurdles would be to gather the families together for a full discussion and the final outcome would not be known for several more weeks.

"So what is it that you thought I had come to help with this morning?" Tye asks his sister. Hosta suspects what his mother might have in mind, and he knows that this day would likely be busy and full.

"It is much past the time to fire my pots," Say announces proudly, "and today is the day I have set aside. Since you two boys are here, you can help."

Hosta's mother is a potter of great skill and ability. Her wares are sought after and the trading parties leaving her village always take a number of her pottery items with them on their trading missions. Say acquired her skill over many years of experimentation, having her share of both suc-cesses and failures. Her own mother had been an excellent potter as well, and although she is too old to continue working, and is nearly blind, she gives Say a lot of helpful advice and support. Many generations ago her family had located a fine deposit of excellent pottery clay near their village. Not only were Say's pots well built, but her unique designs gave her work a pleasant and unique appearance.

Pottery making is mostly a springtime activity, although this year Say has managed to get far behind in her work. First, there was a growing demand for some of her wares, and it was taking a lot of time to gather and process the raw clay. The past year had also been particularly hard on her own supply of storage jars. Two of her large grain storage jars had been broken during the winter, and her favorite corrugated cooking pot had also cracked and was no longer repairable. Several of her best pots from last season had accompanied Koya on his last trip. When all other members of the trading party had returned to the village without him, Say could not allow herself to engage in the pleasant yet intense chore of pottery making.

Over the past several weeks, however, Say managed to complete the decorating of about two dozen bowls, ladles, and mugs, along with some larger water storage jars and cooking pots. These were the items that now required firing, and it was time to get the job done. This final step in the pottery-making process was in many ways the most important. In firing, a number of complex physical and chemical changes take place that assist in converting clay into a hardened substance that will hold its shape and make the material impervious to water. The stresses that occur in the firing process are all too well known to experienced potters, and extreme care must be taken to see that this final but vital step is handled correctly.

Two days ago, Say scooped out a shallow pit about a half mile down the hillside near the spring where she collects water. It was this spot that she and her family had used over the past several years for the firing of their pots. A good supply of wood, bark, and other materials had been collected and stacked nearby over the years. All that would be required now would be to haul her wares down, set out a bed of wood, bark, and wood chips, and begin the firing process. It would be a great deal easier now with her two draftees helping out. And it was a joyful activity for Say and one that she looked forward to.

The making and use of pottery dramatically changed the lives of the people in this region. It had a profound impact on the types and varieties of food that could be prepared and served. A vessel that could be placed directly on a fire led to entirely new diets and preparing a variety of food types. Meat could be cooked in combination with commonly available plants so that a variety of soups and stews could be produced. Along with a more varied and improved diet, the drudgery and lengthy time of food preparation were permanently altered.

Before the introduction and mastery of pottery making, the transportation of water and the storage of food was done using vessels made from natural materials such as gourds. It is no coincidence that the earliest pottery forms looked like the gourds they were designed to replace. Large gourd shapes were used for jars and pitchers, and partial gourd shapes were the inspiration for bowls, plates, and other utilitarian items. Before the widespread use of pottery, baskets served in the preparation of cooked foods and the storage of grains and other items. Heated stones were simply set inside baskets to warm or even cook food.

Pottery was also invaluable for the long-term storage of essential items like grain, and especially water. Baskets were notoriously inefficient for storing water but a number of easily-made pottery vessels could store water in great quantities and for long periods of time. Most of the water storage containers were unglazed, or undecorated, and were quite porous. As some of the water evaporated off the surface of the jar, it helped to keep the water cool and sweet.

Early pottery was made out of pure clay that was easily gathered along the stream beds in many areas throughout the Southwest. But the success of these early attempts at making useful pottery was not entirely satisfactory. Clay alone did not hold its shape well, and became very brittle when fired. But as time and experimentation went on, raw clay was combined with other essential materials that are called "tempers." Sometimes grass or straw was used to temper the raw clay. This did help in the shaping of pottery, but it would easily burn when placed on a fire. Over many years of experimentation, straw and grass were slowly replaced by sand or grit which worked quite well.

Pottery is nothing more than a combination of our planet's most basic materials—earth, water, and fire. Natural clays occur in carbonaceous shale lenses that are found in the sandstones of the Mesa Verde Formation, or from underlying Mancos shales that are found at the foot of cliffs or near canyon walls. There are deposits all throughout the region, some in a natural blue-gray color, some in a red-brown color, and still others in a unique combination of colors. These clays are quite plastic and not too prone to shrinkage when subjected to sudden and rather extreme changes in temperature during the firing process. Some of the clays are better than others, and each of the women has her own special place where she extracts and processes the clay she is most familiar with.

Say, her mother, and a few of the men of the village left their homes in early spring to dig out a quantity of clay from their favorite place. They carried the material back to their village in large baskets. The raw clay is usually quite soft in the early spring and not much additional moisture was needed to process the clay further. In fact, they could quickly spread the clay out in the sun to dry and pick out any foreign materials like stones, twigs, or roots. Once the clay dries thoroughly, they grind it on a metate which is the same kind of flat stone the women use to grind their corn. Sometimes the exact same tool is used although many potters have their own special metate for grinding clay and another for corn.

After drying in the sun, the clay may also be cleaned further by hand or by a process known of as "winnowing." This involves placing a mat, cloth, or buckskin down-wind and simply throwing handfuls of dry clay into the air. The much lighter dried clay is carried by the breeze into the cloth, and any of the larger and heavier impurities fall directly to the ground.

Early tempering materials contained mostly sand or grit, but over the past several hundred years potters like Say have used a different material that is abundant and has proven itself to be an excellent tempering agent. This new and improved temper was produced by grinding down broken pieces of fired pottery. When everyday utensils finally cracked or broke entirely, the pieces of broken pottery were crushed between rocks and then ground even finer on a metate.

Clay and temper are then combined in a recipe of one part temper and two parts clay. The potter thoroughly mixes these dry materials together and only when she is satisfied that a good mix of materials has been made will she add water. She then kneads the resulting paste just like bread dough is kneaded today. This task cannot be done quickly because the mixing and blending of all elements must be thorough and complete.

Say and several potters from the extended family produced a large mass of clay all at once. Then the real work began as Say snipped off an egg-sized chunk of clay in her hands and using her palm rolled it out on a smooth stone. No wheel or other device is used in making pottery and it all simply begins with a long coil of clay that will be continuously rolled out until a length satisfactory to the potter is obtained. The rope of clay is about the diameter of Say's little finger, and she could easily tell when it was ready to work. She picked up the clay from the stone and saw that it held together and had the right elasticity. She started at one end and began to coil the clay around on itself. With each successive coiling she used her thumb and forefinger to pinch the rows of clay coils together.

She rolled out another length of clay and added to it what she had already finished. She added coil after coil until a rough pot emerged. At this point the spiraling of each coil was clearly visible and the prints of her fingers were easily detected on the pinched surface of each coil of the pot. This gave the exterior of the piece the look of being corrugated.

She now had to make a decision. If her pot was to be used for cooking, she would generally retain the rough corrugated appearance on the outside but would smooth the surface on the inside. The pot would be fired without decoration because when used as a cooking pot any decoration would soon be blackened with soot. If her pot was to be used for some other purpose, the coils were more carefully smoothed out as the pot was being shaped. She would make both the outside and inside of her pot equally smooth. Tools, such as pieces of dried gourd or smooth river rocks, would help Say to blend the coils together so that a smooth surface resulted. A small piece of hide was sometimes used later to further smooth the surface of a pot. When all of this work was completed, Say left her pots to dry in the sun. Working with her finer pots, which is Say's favorite activity, required the use of an additional and important ingredient. This other material also comes from the earth and is gathered from a place just under the red topsoil in many areas close by. This white clay is ground on a metate just like the clay from the streambed, and is mixed with water until a soupy mixture results. This soupy clay material is called "slip" and it is applied over the entire surface of a finely crafted pottery piece, which gives many of the sun-dried pots a distinctive white appearance.

Just as the slip began to dry, Say took one of her very smooth river bottom pebbles and rubbed the still-wet slip into the clay body. She used short and brisk strokes over the entire surface where the slip had been applied. The combining of the slip and clay produced a shiny and some-what polished surface. Although a tedious job, it is also important and has a great deal to do with the quality of the finished piece.

Now, the best part for Say began, as she loves to decorate her finer pieces. Using the Beeweed plant—which she has boiled and thickened to a dark brown color, Say picked up one of her many brushes. These brushes are made from small pieces of yucca leaf, one end of which she has chewed to loosen and soften the fibers. Say has several different sizes of these slender leaves and has chosen a mid-sized one to begin work on a nicely-shaped ladle which is one of her recent efforts. The design placed in the bowl of this piece comes freely from her mind. She did not draw the design previously, but the pattern sparks from her own imagination and experience.

Dark tan lines are painted from the opening of her bowl, down toward the center of the piece. At the exact center, she makes three equal horizontal lines completely around the bowl. Now she decides to fill in the spaces between the center lines and the others she has drawn from the opening to the center with a checkerboard pattern.

Say continues working very slowly on this and her other fine pottery pieces. She will often repeat a particular design but tries her best to come up with fresh new ideas. Some of her decorations are very bold and have striking contrast between the dark and light areas. Other designs make use of concentric circles, and some have several parallel lines painted close to one another. At times, she might use very subtle lines in both a horizontal and vertical direction, or a distinctive checkerboard pattern which is one of her favorite designs.

Last year, after one of Koya's trading expeditions, he had brought Say a most unusual pot that had been made somewhere to the south, where his trading party had gone to acquire turquoise, shell, and a variety of colorful feathers. The pot Koya brought home with him had a bright red body with beautiful dark orange and black decoration painted on it. Say thought it was one of the most unusual and one of the prettiest pieces she had ever seen. The entire pot had been made from a red-brown clay, and she wondered if it might be possible to locate that kind of unique clay in the area, or perhaps find the slip material with which the pot had been finished. In any event, she spent many long hours studying this pot, not only because of its unusual and well-executed surface decoration, but because the shape of the pot was very well proportioned and simply felt good when it was held. She showed this object to other potters of her village and they also shared her great admiration of this interesting and unique item. It became a source of renewed inspiration for many of them and the design was sure to appear in the next seasons' production of pottery.

A few years before, Koya had give her another interesting bowl he found on another one of his trading journeys. This particular bowl contained the bold design of a stylized bird and it had been painted right in the middle of the bowl. Around this bird, equally bold geometric designs encircled the outer rim. Say believed it was one of the prettiest and most unusual pieces she had ever seen. The season after receiving it, she tried her hand at making bold designs on a number of her bowls. After some experimentation, Say's fellow potters praised her for all the innovative pottery designs she had produced that year. Her reputation as one of the finest and most creative potters in her village, and in the region, was a source of great pride to Say and to her entire family.

So it was on this pleasant day, after a rather intense morning, that Say, her brother Tye, her oldest son, and the two younger children made their way down to where the fire would be started and the product of her efforts would be finished.

Prehistoric potters did not use an enclosed kiln for firing their pots. What was used is known as a "clamp," or simply a bonfire. Because of not having an enclosed and therefore a concentrated and intense fire, the maximum temperature attainable in an open fire is somewhat limited. Studies conducted by contemporary craftsmen indicate that an open wood fire will produce firing temperatures between 600 and 1000 degrees Centigrade. In modern terms, most Anasazi pottery would be classified as terra cotta because it is fired below 1000 degrees Centigrade. These firing temperatures produce finished wares that are highly porous and not near the hardness of earthenware or stoneware that requires much higher firing temperatures. Thus, the term "pottery" is much more applicable in reference to Anasazi ware than the term "ceramics," which more accurately describes wares that are fired at much higher temperatures.

Everyone waited until Say had placed her pots just as she wanted them before they all began placing fuel around the top of the pit. It was important that Say be satisfied with the arrangement of the pots to be fired, and her knowledge of where the most intense heat would gather was very important in having a successful firing. In order to get the intense heat all around a pot, some fuel would be set under the object to be fired. This required that the pots be supported in some way and thin sandstone slabs, cobbles, or larger pottery sherds were often used for this purpose.

Pots of various types were usually placed together, and she knew from prior experience just how the arrangement of her pots would produce the best results. Hopefully, the pots had dried evenly and thoroughly, because if any air bubbles remained in the clay, or between the coils, they might likely explode during the firing process and entirely destroy her efforts. This happened frequently, although it did provide an abundant source of tempering material for the next season of pot making.

Hosta and Tye set the fuel on fire as the family sat upwind from it to make sure it would not get out of control, and each of them was left to personal thoughts. The younger kids, or course, entertained themselves with running and jumping games. Say and Tye walked a bit further south together and Hosta assumed they were talking over the things that had been discussed earlier this morning. Hosta was anxious to get back to the fields, but because he got so little sleep last night, he decided to take it easy and sit under the shade of a nearby tree. It was another warm and pleasant day, but a few large clouds were collecting to the west. The snapping and sparking of the fire were comforting sounds, and he laid back on the ground and looked up at a bright blue sky. It didn't take long before his mind wandered and he began thinking about a number of important things.

Katti, of course, was the first person to jump into his thoughts. He pictured her, and just knew in his own heart that things would work themselves out. He only hoped that she felt as positively about him as he did for her. What if she had already been spoken for? That was certainly a possibility. It might be that it he was simply too late. It might be that her family had already entered into an agreement with another young man's family somewhere else. Hosta almost jolted upright as this troubling thought came to his mind. He soon relaxed again and thought, no, things were going to be fine. Everything would work out. He thought for a minute about the gift he would make for Katti as part of their marriage contract. Because he had watched his own grandfather weave many fine cotton blankets for so many years, he considered weaving Katti a fine white cotton blanket for her very own. He knew that several of his nephews and cousins would be more than happy to help him in this endeavor. And so that was it. He would weave a beautiful white cotton blanket for his bride-to-be.

Cotton itself was not native to the area where Hosta lived. The nights here were much too cool, but cotton did grow in abundance in the warmer lowlands to the south. Cotton was easily obtained through trade with the people who lived there. His own father had brought back a lot of cotton over the years because it was an item that was easily traded for and most welcomed by the people of his village. It was not likely, however, that enough cotton was currently available for Hosta to start his project, so he had to plan how he might acquire enough to begin the project he felt it was his duty and privilege to make.

Because his father had been a trader for so long, Hosta had acquired a pretty good knowledge about the items that were the most valuable or the most desirable to be traded for in distant areas. He knew, for example, that his father had successfully traded every bow he had personally made and taken on his many trading journeys. It was also certain that Say's pottery was very well accepted because he had never returned home without trading every last one of her fine pots for important things like salt, turquoise, and obsidian.

But there was one item he could remember his father saying was extremely valuable in trade, and always keenly sought whenever and wherever he went. It was the skin of a spotted fawn that was used in many important ceremonies by the people who lived to the south. Deer were quite scarce in many areas to the south, although they were abundant here, and Hosta instantly knew what he would be doing in the next several days. He would use all his hunting skills to kill several spotted fawns so he could use their skins to trade for all the cotton he would need for Katti's blanket. Perhaps there might even be enough cotton left to make his uncle, mother, and Katti's mother something nice as well. The hunting and killing of these fawns would not be easy for a couple of reasons. First, it was pretty late in the season to find a fawn which still had its spots. It wasn't impossible, but it would have been much easier earlier in the spring. More importantly, the animals could not be brought down with bow and arrows. Doing so would lessen the value of the skins. The deer would have to be caught and choked to death by hand without evidence of having their skins penetrated by an arrow. Right now, at this time in the season, many of the deer were moving to higher ground and it would be necessary to track them some distance from the village. But that was all right because Hosta had often hunted with both his uncle and father and knew exactly what would be required to have a successful hunt.

Hosta thought about these things as he drifted between that comfortable place which lies between active thought and the quiet and relaxing nap he could feel coming on. He would plan this hunting trip and ask that his best friend Ika join him in his effort. Just as the thrill and anticipation of this trip drifted through his mind Hosta was jolted back to reality with thoughts about the many things that would be necessary to accomplish before this hunting trip could begin. The families would still need to meet, discuss, and even negotiate the acceptability of his marrying the young lady. Perhaps it was much too early to begin planning anything at all, because a favorable outcome of his desires had not even been started, let alone successfully completed.

Just as Hosta drifted off to sleep, Katti and her mother were busy working on a project they had begun earlier in the spring. At the moment, the two women were finishing the routine of their daily chores that consisted of grinding corn, gathering water, and making sure their house and courtyard were clean. Using bunches of stiff grass that had been tied together with cord, Katti and her mother swept up wind-blown debris and other trash and dumped it in a growing heap directly in front of their home. They also made sure their flock of turkeys didn't stray too far from the surrounding area. Katti's younger sister was playing with a number of her friends near the trash heap and they entertained each other by throwing small pebbles at the noisy turkeys.

Spring is an excellent time for the villagers of this area to do the heavy work of cleaning, repairing, and remodeling their houses. Over the past several years a couple of the walls of Katti's home were showing signs of major settling because cracks would appear, be continually repaired, and then reappear. Katti's mother decided last fall that when spring finally came, it would be time to perform some major repair work. At the same time, she would begin a project she had considered starting for some time and simply never had time to work on.

The cracked walls were most likely the result of natural settling that occurs when a newer house is built on the remains of an earlier habitation site whose foundation wasn't as skillfully constructed as a newer home would be. Sometimes entire homes had to be dismantled and rebuilt because of a faulty foundation, or for some other reason. At other times, new rooms were needed or desired, and villagers were caught up in an endless cycle of repairing, rebuilding, and remodeling.

The project Katti and her mother were currently working on involved re-plastering both the inside and outside their newly remodeled home. Most of this work was done by the women because houses always belonged to them. When there was heavy work to do, the men would be asked to help out. For this particular project new wooden poles had been prepared and put into position by the men, and all of the new foundation stonework had been finished by them. Sometimes stones were used in a project particularly if an entire new foundation was required. The stones were not quarried, but rather easily acquired from around the many canyon rims and rocky slopes in the area. The soft white sandstone was simply picked up off the ground and, using a heavy maul or hammer, they were given a few well-placed blows. In this way the necessary finished shapes and sizes were easily obtained. The men were quite good at this task, having done it for many years. At times, further refinements were made to the stone using small pecking tools or rubbing stones that were used to give a nicely finished appearance to their stonework.

Once this heavy task was completed, the women would take over. Mortar for the walls was prepared and applied by them. As each of the walls was finished, prayer sticks might be buried and plastered over in the corner of each wall. These small sticks are generally hand-carved in various shapes and act as a simple offering to the gods who hopefully will assure both physical and spiritual stability of the house.

Just before the spring planting began this season, the structural work on Katti's house was finished, and she and her mother were now completing the next phase of work that consisted of plastering both the interior and exterior walls of their home. Not all of the houses in their village were plastered both on the outside and the inside, but Katti's mother had a reputation for being an excellent housekeeper and this extra effort gained her a favorable reputation among the other women in her village and beyond. Some of the village women were even quite jealous of Katti's mother, and many said the only reason she worked so hard was that she was trying to impress everyone and help herself find another husband.

The work today was nothing more than a satisfying labor of love for Katti and her mother. Yesterday they finished putting a thin and smooth layer of reddish-brown clay on the interior walls with their bare hands. They were now mixing a batch of clean and chalky-white clay which had the texture and consistency of the slip they used in their pottery making. Once this mixture was just right, Katti's mother grabbed a large yucca brush and began painting over the darker background plaster. A band of the darker color was left about a foot above the floor on each of the four walls, and a similar band about half the thickness was left on the top. In between, bold lines that ran from left to right were painted and then a thinner band of lines ran from top to bottom which made a pyramid shape coming together in groups of three. These designs might also be described as parallel peaks but however one might describe them, they produced a dramatic visual effect against the darker background. The overall effort was quite pleasing, and the two women were very satisfied with what they had created.

Katti worked diligently under her mother's firm but helpful direction. Every now and then some of the thin slip would puddle on the lower edge of a design and Katti would carefully take her finger and run it across the thickening band of clay to make sure the pattern would not run and destroy the evenness of her work. During these rather tedious tasks her mind would wander and her thoughts would often focus on that young man she remembered meeting and the talk she had last evening with his uncle. Maybe this would be a good time to reinforce her strong feelings by discussing her current thoughts with her mother. She thought about saying something and just as quickly dismissed any thought of bringing up the matter now.

Her own family situation was a bit unsettling. Her father was no longer living with them in the village. Several years ago, just after the birth of her younger sister, Katti's father moved back to live with his own clan. Her father was a rather quiet and deliberate man who now lived with his mother and his brothers in dwellings they built in one of the cave-like features down at Mesa Verde. He was a naturally gifted stone mason who loved working with his hands. The people of his own clan were in awe of his talents and abilities, and he even helped build a multi-storied living structure in one of the sandstone caves at Mesa Verde. In fact, in the years to come, his most famous structure would be nearly four stories tall which he helped build at the rear of one of the ledges where he and his family clan now lived. Katti's father had not remained in contact with his family over the past several years. When local trading parties would return to Katti's village from the caves at Mesa Verde, they always provided information of the health and well-being of this man who was now almost completely out of their lives. The divorce was completed with the same swiftness and simplicity as had their marriage. One day several years ago, Katti's father simply took up his personal belongings and moved out of the house and went back to his mother's village. Had Katti's mother been the one to elect to terminate the relationship, she would have waited for him to go on one of his stone-gathering trips, or a hunting expedition, and upon his return he would have found all his worldly possessions sitting in front of the house. He might even have encountered all of his wife's relatives who would have come over to defend the woman's decision. The children, of course, would remain with the woman, as they always belong to the mother's clan.

Katti really doesn't miss her father for she had not spent much time with him anyway. Their village was growing, and there were always things to be built and he had not been around very much in her early years. As friction between her mother and father grew, he spent less and less time around the village so his leaving permanently hardly seemed unusual and Katti thought little about it. There were many men in her village who were always willing and able to provide assistance to her family, and her mother was quite a resourceful and independent woman.

As clouds begin to build in the west, Katti and her mother finish cleaning up the bowls, jars, and other tools they used in their afternoon of decorating. It is almost time to think about getting the evening meal prepared, as the men of the village will soon be coming back from the fields. A special treat is in store for the evening meal as one of the boys of the village managed to snare a couple of nice groundsquirrels in one of the snare traps he had set out yesterday. This boy is one of Katti's cousins and lives close by. He proudly brought over the plump squirrels earlier in the morning and Katti needs to skin and prepare them for the evening meal. It is a chore she knows will be assigned to her, and she smiles to herself recalling how proud her cousin had been this morning when he brought this fresh meat to share with them. It is a wonderfully abundant life and Katti is very satisfied with the way things are going. If she could only get thoughts of that young man Hosta out of her mind, life would be nearly perfect.

Hosta is wrested from his nap by a loud clap of thunder. It is so loud that he nearly jumps up from the ground. His eyes flash wide and he turns to the west from where the thunder has come. A cover of dark clouds hangs in the sky and the warmth that had been in the air is slowly disappearing. Just a few miles west, more lightening can be seen and the deep roll of thunder is heard once again.

Tye and Say are bending over the smoldering remains of their fire knocking away some of the hot coals that can be seen beside the pit. A few of Say's smaller pots, which have already cooled enough to pick up, are sitting on the side of the fire pit. It is going to be necessary to work quickly now as the approaching storm might bring rains heavy enough that they could easily damage the newly-fired pots. Hosta jumps to his feet and joins the others to offer whatever assistance he can. Sticks are the primary tool used to remove pots from the pit. Jars and pitchers are the easiest to lift out because a stick can be inserted into one end and simply lifted. It is the bowls and ladles that are a bit more difficult to remove. Using two sticks, one in each hand, Say carefully works under and around the piece, lifting and carrying it out of harm's way. From time to time, a pot or bowl has exploded during the firing process and is simply left in the pit so that the other more valuable objects can be retrieved. At this point many of Say's fine surface decorations are not in evidence. Only after the pots have cooled will she be able to wipe them clean and perhaps wash them with water or even wipe them with an oil so the designs she so skillfully painted will be fully revealed. Firing is perhaps the most interesting and the absolute best time for Say as each of her pots will fire in its own unique way and the final process is never possible to fully control. Many times a piece will be a complete disappointment. At other times a nicely decorated pot will quite unexpectedly come out splendidly and give its creator a great sense of accomplishment and pride.

They move most of the pots taken from the fire pit today to a place under a rock outcropping to provide shelter from any rain that might come. These pots will be carried back home some time later. The three of them will carry home a few of the smaller and more interesting pieces, and once they climb the last small hill, careful not to drop anything, they quickly enter the house.

The light breeze has suddenly stopped and within minutes rain begins to fall. It strikes some dust right outside their door. Big drops hit the earth and briefly hang in suspension before being absorbed into the fine dirt to become a tiny clump of mud. It is getting to be that time in the month when rains will be more frequent although mainly in the afternoon. These storms will last for an hour or so. Sometimes it will rain heavily, but the real rainy season is several weeks away. This gentle rain comes at a good time because the fields need any moisture they can obtain from any source.

Throughout the region many small ponds have been built to store precious water from much larger ponds that also have been built by hand. Water for each of these ponds has been diverted from small steams which run along the canyons, and over the last couple of weeks these streams were getting smaller and smaller. If these early-summer rains had not come, more work would need to be done to ensure that moisture would reach the nearby fields. It is a welcome relief to see these late afternoon rains. It is certain that the Rain Men from the villages have been successful in performing their dances and rituals and it is reassuring to know that the evil witches have once been overcome, at least up until now, and that the gods are looking kindly on the people.

As the rains continue coming down, Say takes one of the ladles she has brought with her and turns it over repeatedly in her hands. As she admires how nicely balanced the item has turned out, she carefully wipes the handle that is covered with soot and then wipes out the ladle's bowl. She slowly dips it into a jar of water and continues removing the fine soot and a little caked-on debris. She is quite happy with this particular piece and it is one of the items she has decorated with her newest batch of Beeweed pigment and her newest yucca brush.

She admires the ladle's interior design that consists of an inside band of deep black color about a half-inch wide which runs completely around the top inside the bowl. Three smaller bands of dark color are parallel to the top band and a final larger band is close to the center of the bowl. A geometric pattern consisting of three dark lines that look like a series of capital "C"s and intertwine one another. In the center of this design is a smaller box-like design. Around the outside rim of the bowl are dark lines spaced about a half inch apart. The handle of the ladle is nicely decorated with a pattern that repeats the interior design of the bowl. A larger half-inch band runs down the middle, on each side, and on the bottom of the handle. Between these larger patterns, thinner and more intricate parallel lines run to the center of the handle and are interconnected with smaller lines.

Say sets this ladle aside, glancing at the two men who are watching her. "I think this is a nice one, and I might have to use it as a gift sometime in the near future, so don't you go using it for anything, all right?"

Hosta glances over at Tye, smiles quickly and says, "Sure, Mom. I know the gift will be very much appreciated."

Tye smiles back, giving him some encouragement that his mother is quickly accepting an important change in all of their lives.

CHAPTER six

When the afternoon rains stop, the men walk back into their fields to determine if the wind and rain caused any damage. Here and there small earthen check dams might have given way and would need to be repaired. Sometimes wind-blown debris would be carried into the fields and would need to be removed. Because the earth is now softened, a more effective job of weeding could begin. This task starts in the spring well before crops are planted and continues until the crops are harvested later in the fall.

Another critical task of the farmers is to thin their crops. Weaker stalks of corn must be pulled out so that they will not compete for precious moisture with stronger and better producers of a good harvest. There is hardly a time that the fields do not require the care and attention of these farmers, but that doesn't mean there isn't time to do other useful tasks as well.

As the growing season continues, and the crops flourish, every man is also involved in producing goods that will be used in everyday life, or is engaged in producing goods that can be traded for other useful items. Almost all of the men are capable of making goods they need for everyday life, although some excel in certain skills. In one of the village houses a man makes excellent arrowheads and produces them in abundance both for his own use and for trade. In another house an older man is a well-known weaver whose cotton blankets are greatly admired and sought. Down the path there is a stone ax maker whose wares are greatly appreciated and easy to trade. Another man has learned the fine art of tanning buckskins. Yet another can weave yucca fibers into very fine cords and ropes. There is even a jeweler in the village who makes many fine ornaments from the colorful and exotic materials that he has traded for throughout the region. Because of this semi-specialization of the village men, there is an abundance of items that they use in trading. Trade is one of the most important activities that takes place during the warm-weather months of spring and summer.

Foot trails link one village to another. When time is available, several men join together and make their way to other villages to trade for stone knives, interesting and colorful stones and rocks, and salt, which is one of the most precious trade items of all. Traders come to Hosta's village from areas both near and far away. This activity continues throughout the season and information may be one of the most valuable and important traded commodities of all. Information is obtained and exchanged about a variety of things and often includes news about the well-being of crops in other areas, hunting conditions in different parts of the region, and other news, both good and bad. It was recently learned, for example, that a village not far away has been hit by a form of dysentery and many of the children of that village have died. It has been learned that somewhere to the south a plague of grasshoppers recently destroyed many of the area's crops. Up near the big mountains, a forest fire was started by lightning, destroying several villages and killing many people. Other news may bring word of a fine crop of pinyon nuts, or that a huge deer population has been spotted not far from where the forest fire is raging. Recent information brings word of a newly discovered vein of excellent quality turquoise. In a village near Mesa Verde, a woman has given birth to twins, and a man has been murdered by an unknown assailant, and the murder still remains a mystery. One of the medicine men is treating a chief for a very bad skin condition and is reported to be having great success with using a combination of new varieties of healing herbs along with ceremonial chanting.

There is always great interest in knowing about enemy raiders. Listening becomes very focused when talk about these enemy raiders begins. These raiders are people who are possessed by witches and whose mission is to harm and kill the people. The threat of enemy invaders has been talked about for generations and although neither Hosta nor Katti's village has suffered, stories are told about entire villages that have been destroyed by these evil and treacherous people. The storytellers also speak about the stealing of women and the destruction of crops, and everyone listens intently when these stories of enemy raiders are told and retold.

When trading parties come to a village they are treated as special guests. In fact, these visits often become an excuse for extended festivities that include the lengthy preparation of many fine dishes. At meal time, traders are given a bowl and asked to join in the evening's repast with all members of a family. Sometimes they are invited to spend the night, but many traders simply want to finish with their drawn-out negotiations and begin moving on to the next village.

It was just after one of these trading visits that a family council meeting is being held by Hosta's clan. All family members listen intently as Say presents everyone with important information concerning her oldest son who wishes to marry a young lady by the name of Katti, who is a member of the Water Clan, and who Say believes would make a wonderful addition to the family. Hosta is not invited to participate in this important discussion and he spends most of the night in the fields trying to walk off his nervous energy.

Later in the evening he comes back to his village and is greeted by Tye who holds out both hands to his nephew and says, "Tomorrow, we will all go to visit with the young lady's family. If they agree to allow Katti to be your bride, we would all be pleased to welcome her into our family."

Hosta can barely contain his pleasure in hearing the news. He rushes into the house and embraces his mother, telling her how pleased he is to hear about the family's acceptance of his plan.

"I am only sad that father is not able to hear this good news," Hosta says to everyone, "but I know that he also would approve of your decision."

Everyone present pauses to reflect on what has been said and is saddened that Koya is not able to participate in their happiness.

The following day many family members pay a visit to Katti's village and her people. Both of the villages are aware that this visit will take place because Katti's mother could not contain herself and had already spoken with several of her clan. Most everyone already knows that Hosta's family will be coming to discuss this important matter and there was great anticipation among all the villagers. Katti was very pleased after she shared her feelings and concerns with her mother. Not only had she accepted the news but hugged her oldest daughter to give assurance that she would do everything possible to see that the clan members would support her daughter's desire to marry.

The family meeting takes place outdoors in the plaza area of Katti's village. Elders, priests, and other dignitaries of the clan are present to discuss and negotiate the many details of the proposed marriage. It takes the better part of an afternoon, but finally all details are agreed upon. The news is conveyed to Katti by her mother, who asks that Hosta and his family join them for that evening's meal.

A ceremony of sorts takes place that night with Hosta and Katti the center of attention. They blush as this attention is bestowed on them. They sit together and hold hands and are too engrossed in one another to be hungry. While some of the clan start to eat and tell stories, others rejoice in the events they are planning together. As their attention is diverted, the two young people quietly steal away just after the sun sets. They go to a place near the fields in order to quietly express their love and devotion to one another and have time to discuss the life they will soon begin to share together.

As the summer continues, Katti's family is busily engaged in making preparations for building the home in which the new couple will live. It is always the responsibility of the young lady's family to build a home for the couple-to-be. It will not take long to complete this project, as many in Katti's clan are expert builders and have helped to do this kind of task many times before. A surprise is waiting for the family one late summer afternoon.

Right after a site on which the new home will be built has been located and cleared, a stranger comes walking toward the family members. As he approaches, no one can quite make out who he is. As he comes closer, they stare in amazement because it is Katti's father.

He slowly greets everyone and later tells them the story of a trader who has recently come to Mesa Verde and spoke of an impending marriage that included the name of a young girl known as Katti. He listened to this story carefully and felt there was little doubt it was his very own daughter they were speaking of. Because he knew that a house would need to be built, and because he was feeling some remorse at not having visited his family for such a long time, he decided that he would come back and volunteer his services in helping build a new home for his daughter and her new husband. He is, after all, a good stonemason and feels it is the least he can do to help his family.

At first, everyone is a bit uncomfortable having him back among the family, but before long gratitude is expressed concerning his desire to more fully participate in his daughter's new life. Katti herself is quite cautious at first, but becomes very appreciative of her father's having come back to help. She comes to understand that this may be his way of expressing a desire to keep in closer contact with his family. Although no one expects this to be any kind of long-term reconciliation, everyone expresses gratitude that he has come to help in the building of this new home.

Meanwhile, Hosta is making plans to begin his trip into the high country to hunt the spotted deer. He visits Ika soon after the meeting with Katti's family, and tells his best friend what is happening. Ika could not be more pleased for his friend, and offers whatever assistance he can. During this conversation Hosta tells Ika of his desire to weave a white cotton blanket for his bride-to-be, and tells how he intends to trade the skins of spotted fawns for the cotton he needs for the weaving. Ika quickly agrees to help with the hunting plans.

"It's set then," Hosta says. "We will leave in two days' time for the mountains. It will be a great trip for both of us, and I know we will succeed in bringing back many deer."

Both boys are excellent hunters, having first learned at a very young age how to snare smaller game like chipmunks, squirrels, and rats. As they grew older, their fathers and uncles showed them how to use bow and arrows, and taught these youngsters the fine art of stalking larger prey.

Dates for organized hunts in which all members of a village participate are set by a Hunt Chief. These hunts mainly take place in the fall which is a very busy time for all members of the villages.

The men are responsible for the hunt itself, but when the hunting parties return, any game is turned over to the women and girls. It is their responsibility to skin the animals and cut the meat into long strips which is then dried by placing it on long strings tied between house walls and across roof beams or even nearby trees. Throughout the hunting season most of the houses have drying meat hanging everywhere out-of-doors.

There is little waste when making use of the hunter's bounty. All of the meat and organs are eaten or prepared for later use and the hides are tanned and used in making winter clothing. Sinews are used for making bow strings and for sewing hides together. Most of the tanning produces skins that are a soft white leather. Even the bones are used for tools and for making gaming tokens or decorative items that are worn throughout the year. Using bone awls and needles, the women sew skins together with yucca fiber or even cotton string to produce wonderfully useful robes. From time to time a sleeveless slipover buckskin jacket is made, but loose robes that simply hang over the shoulders are preferred by most of the people.

Just before making their trip to the mountains, Hosta and Ika consult with Tye. He is currently engaged in studying the ways of a Hunt Chief and hopes to one day become a Chief himself. Because of Tye's extensive knowledge and his skills in teaching, Hosta specifically wants to consult with him before making the hunting trip. He would also like to obtain a special blessing from the current Hunt Chief for the upcoming trip. Tye has already indicated a willingness to help Hosta in any way that he can so on the evening before the hunting trip is to begin, Hosta and Ika pay a visit to Tye where a special surprise awaits them.

"I talked with the Hunt Chief today," Tye tells the two young men, "and he has agreed to say a special prayer for both of you."

Before each of the traditional hunting trips each fall, a number of ceremonies are held in one of the main ceremonial kivas of the village. It is there that the Hunt Chief, and perhaps several other men endowed with special powers, provide chants or dances in preparation for the upcoming hunting activities. If anyone neglects participating in these important ceremonies, the hunt or an individual hunter might not be successful. Because Hosta and Ika will be hunting on their own, without benefit of others from the village, the Hunt Chief was asked to offer a special prayer for the boys. This was being done as a special favor for Tye, and it is a great honor to be given special consideration for a trip.

"That's great," Hosta says. "We're very appreciative of the Hunt Chief's prayers."

"I have two other surprises for you," Tye says as he reaches down to retrieve something from a small leather pouch.

Hosta and Ika glance at each other wondering what more could be expected from this kind and thoughtful person. Tye takes the small pouch and opens it. What he pulls out make the boys' eyes widen in excitement.

In the palm of his hand, Tye holds two perfectly polished stones, no doubt taken from one of the mesas to the south. They had been carved and finished in such a way that they looked like tiny mountain lions.

"The lion is an excellent hunter. When you each carry one of these with you, it will help give you the strength of a lion and also help give you the skill of a mountain lion who wisely stalks and brings down its prey. I hope the two of you will be successful in your quest, and these are my gifts to you," Tye says.

Each boy takes one of the stone images and holds it in his hand.

"Thank you, Uncle Tye," Hosta says, nearly choked up with gratitude.

"Yah, thanks a lot," repeats Ika. "I promise to keep this with me forever."

"I have one more surprise for the two of you, although it's really a favor that I ask on behalf of the Hunt Chief," Tye says. "You are asked to have a companion accompany you on your hunting trip tomorrow."

Hosta and Ika again look at each other wondering who this unexpected companion might be.

"The Hunt Chief's nephew is Tokana who has just entered the kiva under the sponsorship of his ceremonial father. He has fourteen seasons now, and the young man is very strong and more than able to take care of himself. In fact, Ika, you know him because he lives not far from your village."

"Yes, I know Tokana," Ika responds. "He's a nice kid, and as long as he does as he's told, it will be fine having him along."

"Sure," Hosta replies less enthusiastically. "We will be glad to have him come with us." It is a small price to pay to satisfy the wishes of his uncle and the Hunt Chief and for all the things that have been given to him on this very special day.

Arrangements are made to pick up Tokana on their way to the mountains at first light the next morning. The boys review the items they will need to take with them and discuss the strategy they will employ over the next several days of their hunting expedition.

The many villages in this area of the Four Corners region rest on the mesa tops of an extensive regional drainage system. With the view of an eagle flying overhead, one can see these mesas protrude like fingers and branch generally in an east-to-west direction. Between the fingers are many canyons consisting of rocky walls and ledges that give life to a wide variety of vegetation including trees and bushes from which a bounty of foods and other vital materials can be gathered. At the bottom of each canyon many large and small streams run full during the early spring and again in the late summer rainy season. During the many dry periods in between, these stream beds provide a convenient pathway for both man and animals as they migrate throughout the region.

The mesas are generally at the same elevation throughout the drainage system although the land begins to climb gradually to the west where distinct mountains rise. It can take several days to reach the foothills of these mountains, but as the land begins its gentle climb, both the landscape and the vegetation change. Juniper, pine, and pinyon trees become more plentiful. The ground becomes more cluttered with rock and loose stones, and there are huge rock out-croppings that often run for miles. The canyons become wider and deeper as the land moves away from the mountains, and the streams collect and run more water as they move away from the high range of mountains.

It is over this extensive drainage system that the three young hunters are now walking. They began their journey just before sunrise this morning. Hosta could not wait for the trip to begin and arrived at Ika's village just as the pink light of morning painted a nearly cloudless sky in the east. Hosta gave the low whistle of a bird that was the signal for Ika to join him. In less than a minute the two were off to pick up Tokana and begin their journey.

"Your Uncle Tye is such a great guy," Ika whispers as the two walked toward Tokana's village. "I will keep that hunting fetish with me forever."

"He is a great guy, and some day I hope to repay his kindness in some way. I only hope I will be a good uncle to any nephews I might have one day," Hosta replies.

The increasing light of day brings a brightness to the land as the three young men move quietly toward their objective. From time to time they stop and listen to the many sounds that can be heard along the way, from the fluttering wings of birds to the slight rustle of rabbits scampering around in the brush.

During the regular fall hunting season, larger hunting parties of men split into two or more groups and move between canyons which often run parallel to one another. As the parties move in the same direction, they give each other various aural signals and at the right time they swarm up and out of the canyons to form a wide circle up to a mile in diameter. They begin to chant and shout and make as much noise and commotion as they can. Any game, which might include deer, mountain sheep, foxes, coyotes, and rabbits, quickly becomes surrounded by the ever-tightening circle of hunters. Using this technique concentrates the game in one area and provides the hunters with a great advantage. As the frightened animals dash about in a state of panic and confusion, the animals are encircled by the hunters which greatly improves the productivity of the hunting party. Arrows and clubs bring down the prey but the hunters are always careful not to kill too many of the animals. Their skills and abilities make them capable of capturing tremendous amounts of game, but over the years they have learned to take only as much as they feel is necessary. The land is clearly abundant but it would never serve them well to simply slaughter the animals. Many animals are spared so that they can reproduce in even greater numbers for the hunting seasons to come.

Because this particular hunting trip is special, and because of the specialized techniques they will employ, these hunters are not only looking for a particular type of game but looking in an area that will allow them to track their prey more easily and over greater distances. As they move to higher and higher ground, the hunters stop more frequently to listen and observe their surroundings.

As the sun moves higher and is now nearly overhead, the hunters stop suddenly, kneel down, and look in unison to the west. They see a dozen or more deer in the distance grazing just beyond a rock outcropping where the ground looks wet and matted. This suggests that a spring is nearby and the animals here now likely use this area quite frequently. Without making a sound, Hosta motions to his companions to stay low and move quietly forward to get a better look at the small herd. They are looking specifically for younger animals, hoping they might find one or more spotted fawns in the herd. They cannot see any from their current vantage point, so they move slowly and quietly forward to get a better look at the site.

As they move closer, one of the older females quickly lifts her head and points her ears toward the hunters. She stands as still as a statue then moves her ears and twitches her nose at the same time. She seems to take note of something moving, and doesn't move quickly or in panic but she turns her backside toward the hunters and slowly starts to move away. Many others in the herd do likewise, moving without panic but with a sense that someone in the group might have seen or heard something. It was a signal for the herd to remain on alert.

The hunters stop immediately and watch the herd slowly move away. There is no particular hurry for the hunters to do anything other than carefully search for what they are seeking. So far, they have not clearly determined that any spotted fawns are in this particular herd although one or two of the deer look quite small and possibly were born quite recently.

Again without saying a word, but with simple gestures to one another, the hunters move in the general direction that the deer are moving. They make some mental notes about this place because it has all the elements of being an important gathering place for animals. Not far ahead they note evidence of other hunters having been in the area. There are blood-stained bones, tufts of fur, and surface discoloration, indicating that a pack of coyotes or wolves has feasted on one or more deer not long ago. All these signs point to a good hunting site that will be worth telling the Hunt Chief about for the upcoming season. The young hunters instinctively catalog this place in their minds, memorizing the landscape features that will be useful when trying to find this place again.

They continue tracking their prey and observe several small herds of deer and other game along the way, but so far have not seen the prey they are seeking. Perhaps they will need to move further up to higher ground. Then again, it might be so late in the season they will not be successful in finding what they have come for.

After moving down and across a canyon where a small stream produces a trickle of clear and sparking water, the boys sit down to take a short rest.

"Maybe we should head more into the forest from here," Ika volunteers.

"What do you think, Tokana? Should we keep going down this canyon or head up the other side and go further to the big mountain?" Hosta asks.

Tokana is a young man of few words and doesn't reply with anything more than his eagerness. "I think we should keep going down this canyon. We will find what we're looking for, but the deer won't come to us. We must find them." With this statement and its expression of frustration, the three quickly get up and start walking down the canyon.

About a mile away, and just as the canyon opens and takes a slight angle to the left, Hosta stops suddenly and holds out his right arm. He turns to his two companions and points straight ahead. There, in a clump of deep brush, are a half-dozen deer. Two of them are small but cannot be seen entirely from this angle. As the boys move ahead very slowly, they smile at the sight before them. Two beautifully spotted fawns are seen grazing with their mother. The doe is a beautiful creature with a light tan body and a bright white tail. She is a distinctive-looking animal, as most of the other deer in this region are much darker in color.

As they had discussed before making the trip, the three quickly split up with Ika moving to the right side of the small herd and Tokana moving quickly to the left. Their game-plan is quite simple. They will surround and then begin a long process of stalking their prey. The hunters could easily work themselves into a position where bow and arrows would bring down any number of the animals, but this is not their plan. Because the skin of these deer is to be used in trade and for ceremonial purposes, they will need to stalk the animals until they are either so tired, or so frightened, that it will be easy for these young hunters to run down their prey and choke the animals to death.

If a deer senses that it is being pursued it becomes too nervous to eat or drink. This happens especially when the hunters make sounds and imitate the cries of coyotes or wolves. With all this anxiety building, the younger animals often become separated from their mothers. As they continue to run, they become even more frightened. Because of the lack of nourishment and water, deer will ultimately exhaust themselves and make easy prey for the cunning hunters.

After about ten minutes Hosta hears the cry of a coyote made by one of his companions. Immediately, the deer all raise their heads and look in the direction of the cry. Just as they begin to move in the opposite direction, another similar cry is heard. The animals again move in unison, and start moving down the canyon toward where Hosta has placed himself against a canyon wall. He jumps away from the wall and repeats the sound of a menacing coyote. The deer are in total disarray. Some stop quickly and turn to move back where they had originally been. The spotted fawns anxiously try to stay with their mother, and in the total confusion the herd kicks up clouds of dust as they run and jump over the rock outcropping. They try to move away from the frightening sounds and scamper up the sides of the steep canyon walls.

The hunters continue making as much noise as possible and move to surround the fleeing animals. They know this initial action will produce nothing more than confusion and concern among the herd, but this is neither the time nor the place for their hunt to be concluded. It is, in fact, just beginning.

Moving together the young hunters move quickly to where they suspect their prey is fleeing. The trees begin to thicken as they run toward the fleeing deer and it takes care and agility to move among the trees without stumbling. The boys keep themselves separated but close enough to each other so that if necessary, they could work in unison and quickly encircle the deer once they get closer.

The tracking continues for several hours. The heat of the day is beginning to wane and the hunters walk a bit slower and listen closely as they continue. They sense that the deer are not far away, although they have not spotted them for the past several hours or so. Freshly broken branches and disturbed soil are signs that indicate they are somewhere close. Then, just ahead near a rock outcropping, and under a thick cover of pinyon trees, Ika is the first to spot the herd. It appears as though their numbers have grown considerably larger. The smaller herd has joined up with a larger group of deer that is congregating near a large rock outcropping. The two spotted fawns seem more restless than the others and they and their mother anxiously seek the comfort and security of their group. The larger herd seems to be content and continues to graze without paying much attention to the new arrivals. As this tranquil scene continues before them, the hunters again quietly move to encircle the herd.

Within minutes the single cry of a coyote penetrates the stillness. The animals immediately lift their heads in unison. The fawns are the first to bolt from the area. Once again the deer disperse quickly, running directly away from the sound. Immediately another coyote cry is heard in the direction toward which they are running, and the herd again splits apart. The spotted fawns try to catch up with their mother. The larger group races in a completely different direction, and it will now be possible for the hunters to track the original group with ease.

The deer moves quickly out of sight but the hunters know the general direction in which they are heading. The sun slides behind a gathering bank of clouds, and the air becomes cooler as the long day progresses. It is unlikely that enough time remains to continue tracking the deer and try to bring them down today. The hunters' strategy will be to continue stalking the animals, determine their location, and then try for a kill when the new day comes.

Just as the light of this day dims even more, the three hunters locate their quarry, huddled close to one another among some deep brush just on the edge of a thicker stand of pine trees. The deer seem to be agitated and keep their heads held high looking in all directions at once. Their ears and noses move incessantly, a sign that their intensity of concern hasn't diminished.

The young hunters move together instinctively making sure they remain downwind from the animals so that both their sounds and scent will not spook the herd and cause them to move further away during the descending darkness. With quiet whispers and hand signals the boys decide to make a night of it under a rock outcropping where they can keep their eye on things and try to get some rest before the new day begins.

Throughout the night, they listen to the cries of real coyotes and wolves. They know that these sounds of the night will be sure to keep the deer alert and agitated and add to their growing sense of fear.

As the light of a new morning emerges, Hosta is the first to stir. He moves slowly trying to see if the deer have moved away from the place where they congregated last night. Although the light is dim, he notices movement in the distance. The deer are still there, and he makes his way back to the others still asleep at the place they have camped for the night.

"Ika, the deer have not moved," Hosta whispers directly into the ear of his friend.

Ika's eyes snap open, but he lies quietly on the ground not moving.

"I think this will be the day we bring down our spotted fawns, so we should be ready to move as soon as the sun rises."

Ika nods his head in response. Hosta now moves over to where Tokana sleeps and shakes him gently. He passes on the same message, and the three hunters lie perfectly still, each enjoying his own thoughts as the sun begins to rise in the east.

Their strategy has not changed. Ika gets up and moves around to the left with the intention of placing himself a good distance from the others and waiting for the sounds of his companions once again to spook the herd. Tokana moves to the other side, also awaiting the crying sound of a coyote that Hosta will make as a signal to again begin chasing the deer out into the open.

Over the next half-hour, as the light gains in intensity and strength, Hosta has moved in closer to the herd. He makes the loud cry of a coyote, and the process begins again. The deer move away quickly only to stop suddenly when another cry is heard coming from the direction in which they are running. They turn quickly in the opposite direction and yet another cry is heard. The deer are now in a complete state of panic and begin to run in every direction. The instinctive goal of self-preservation has taken over and each animal is intent on defending itself, forgetting that there is strength in numbers and a common goal of group preservation. Hosta keeps his eyes on one of the spotted fawns that has broken free and runs almost directly toward him. He begins the final process of stalking this animal knowing that it probably spent a very restless night, and in its anxiety has not eaten or gained much strength.

The stalking continues for a couple of hours. Hosta has no idea where his companions are at the moment, and doesn't much care. He is totally focused on the task at hand. He is slightly crouched down, and believes he can hear his prey in the underbrush just ahead. He stops to listen. Just ahead, he sees the fawn against the green background of underbrush and trees. The animal is frightened and it stumbles as it moves. This is a good sign to Hosta, as the animal is weakened from fright and is burning up whatever energy it has left while in its preservation mode.

The deer senses something. Hosta lets out a cry, and the deer springs into action. It moves quickly away from Hosta who begins to run along parallel to the running deer. This chase continues for nearly half an hour, and Hosta is getting winded from the effort and from his own growing sense of anxiety and anticipation.

The deer has stopped once again just ahead. Hosta stops. He gathers strength, takes a number of deep breaths and then runs directly toward the fawn. Its eyes widen, ears flap back, and it turns around to run directly away from this approaching menace. Its heart beats quickly and strongly. Every muscle in its body moves as quickly as it can, but too much of its energy has already been used up. The animal moves, but not as quickly as the young man in pursuit. Hosta and the fawn are in a chase of death. Hosta is running as fast as he can and senses he is closing in on the distance between himself and the fawn. The deer is now directly in front of him. They run together under some trees in an area that has many larger rocks and cobbles on the ground. It is a hard run, and Hosta stumbles over one of the rocks. But the deer is losing whatever remaining energy it has. The fawn now pauses for just an instant, but an instant too long. Hosta is in a dead run raising his hands and ready to leap out at the slowing animal.

Just at this instant, the fawn stops completely. It senses it has lost its remaining ability to escape. It just stops, and turns toward its approaching enemy. In the same fraction of a second, Hosta's right foot hits a soft place on the ground. His right ankle turns in on itself, and he falls forward striking the lower part of his right leg hard on a rock that is protruding out of the ground. As his hands thrust forward to catch his fall, the fawn is within inches of him. Hosta reaches out his arms to encircle the fawn's head and neck.

Hosta lets out a scream of pain. He puts all the weight of his body into trying to wrestle the fawn to the ground. Both of them are now on the ground, Hosta tightly wrapping his right arm around the fawn's neck, and twisting its neck around as the fawn's legs kick in the air. Hosta's pain is almost unbearable as he holds the fawn tighter and tighter to himself, slowly squeezing the life out of the animal. It is almost as though Hosta gains strength from his anger and takes his revenge out on the animal that has caused him to trip and suffer so much pain. As the life slowly drains from his prey, Hosta grits his teeth, lets out a series of moans, and yet never lets go. Quite slowly at first and then almost in an instant the spotted fawn lies still. Its nearly lifeless body quivers briefly and then is totally still. Awash in excruciating pain, Hosta allows himself to slowly let go. He unwraps his arms from around the deer's neck and reaches both hands down to his right leg. He curls up his leg while lying on his back, and continues to grimace in pain. Combined with the pain is exhaustion and excitement all blending together. Hosta has little memory of what happens next. His mind shuts out all but the pain and the meaning of what had happened all so very quickly in the last few minutes.

As he lies on the ground, looking up at the cloudless blue sky, he loses consciousness and is taken to a place where he feels neither pain nor exhilaration. For how long this complete escape from reality will continue, Hosta would never know. He feels nothing at all.

CHAPTER
seven

Somewhere between the conscious world and that often turbulent, problematic, sometimes comforting awareness of reality, a man's thoughts turn to a combination of precise problem-solving and complete nonsense. An exchange of dreamlike vision gives way to images of heroic behavior, transported images of time and space, where fantasy and reality mix to create an intoxicating cocktail of transported thoughts and images.

As reality gains an upper hand in this contest of mental agility, bodily awareness takes hold.

"Ouch, that hurts," I said quietly to myself and grabbed my right calf muscle. The "Charley horse" felt like a hard mass beneath my two hands and I bent the toes of my right foot ever higher toward me. I tightened my eyelids in concert with the pain, trying not to cry out and wake Diane who was very much asleep across the way. I continued to massage the hard knot in my calf, and slowly, ever so slowly, the muscle relaxed and I was able to bend my toes forward and help release the tension and pain.

With that maddening episode over, I was more awake than I either wanted or had intended to be. It was probably all that hunkering down inside the hole and the unexpected burst of physical activity that had caused my body to give me signal that it wasn't as young as it used to be. I had been in decent shape only once in my life, and that was about thirty years ago while attending college. All the intervening years of office work and the absence of much continuing physical activity had not created a specimen whose main challenge in life would be vigorous daily physical activity.

The sun had not yet risen. I peered out through the over-cab window and could see the lights of Cortez in the distance just beginning to dim against a brightening sky. I guessed it was about six in the morning, perhaps a bit earlier. I wondered if I should try to get back to sleep and rest up, or just give in and start the day early. The easiest thing to do was massage the remaining stiffness out of my right calf and then roll over and try to fall back to sleep. But it didn't work. There was too much to look forward to that day. We were nearly halfway through our intended digging activity, and there were a number of interesting things happening. I wanted the day to begin, and was sorry it wasn't later and that things weren't already happening.

I decided to get up. I put on a pair of jeans, and threw on a long-sleeved sweatshirt as it was typically cool in the morning. I pushed on my filthy but once-white sneakers and as quietly as possible sneaked out the door.

It was another glorious cloudless morning. The brightness to the east gave warning that the sun would rise over the San Juans any minute now. "God, I wish I had a cup of coffee," I thought, but as opposed to craving one, I started walking up toward the site.

Just as I arrived the first light of morning switched on in the eastern sky. I stood back for a moment taking it all in. Over the six upright poles hung our sun screen, and the morning light spread across the excavation we had created over the last several days. I walked slowly up the rise, and peered in that deepening hole in the ground and looked down at the bench where I found the two ladles yesterday. I moved around to the other side, looking directly at the rising sun, and peered down at the ten-by-ten-meter section we would be digging into today. What more might lay beneath was anyone's guess. Perhaps more of Pat would be found, perhaps the kiva floor would begin to emerge on this day. I stood so close to the edge that a bit of loose soil dropped down into the hole. I stepped back quickly and walked over to the area Kelly had been working on yesterday. In doing this I had a vision of the area having upright wooden poles that once enclosed a living or storage space now over a thousand years old. My right calf was still a bit tight as I bent down on my knees and slowly sat on the ground.

I looked all around the site first toward the midden area to the south. It would be interesting when we had time to cut a trench across that area and uncover the many items these ancient people considered to be no longer useful to them and simply threw away. What someone a thousand years before might consider no longer necessary would prove completely intriguing to us today.

As I glanced back to the east, I looked across a wide-open area that most recently had been grazing land. Were these fields once full of corn and squash and beans, planted by these ancient inhabitants who are long vanished from here? Could I make out the tops of growing maize shimmering in the midsummer sun of a new day, and were the two rabbits I saw running across the field being chased away by the farmers who would just now be coming into their fields for another day of work?

Could the smoke from their evening fire be the scent in the air this morning, or was it from one of the many underbrush fires that Edmund and Cecil had set yesterday in their continuing process of cleaning up?

I had thoughts about a number of activities that might have happened around me as I sat and considered the lives of the people who had been here long before me. Although we exist differently in time and space, we were all part of the fabric of human activity that has ennobled this place over the centuries. Each of us is involved with this place to the extent that our current technology and ingenuity allows. We individually work and produce on this land in ways that are entirely different and yet oddly similar. In a thousand years, I wondered if anyone else would care about what we were doing here on this very day. Would anyone else be as curious as I was this morning to discover what life was like two thousand years before? No one knows the answer, but as long as human curiosity and the pursuit of knowledge exist, one would expect that this place will continue to be explored over a vast expanse of time. As each generation grows in its use of technology it is more and more likely that so much more will be known about this place and about how man lived here over such a great span of time.

I walked back to the motor home for that long-awaited cup of coffee. Right after I lit the stove it wasn't long before Diane began to rise and begin her morning rituals. It wasn't long before we heard the crew drive up to the site, and it was time once again to begin the day's work.

When we arrived at the site, Kelly was busy working on her portion of the project and Kay was setting up the transit. With coffee cup in hand, and Diane trailing not far behind, I joined the crew and exchanged morning greetings.

"Talked with Jerry this morning, and he'll be coming down a bit later on," Kay reported. "He's going up to the other site to check things out before coming here."

The site Kay referred to was about a quarter mile northwest of our project. Earlier in the spring Jerry and his crew had started work on excavating another kiva that had been discovered on Archie Hanson's out-lot. This lot was located just to the south of the main road intersection that led to a driveway and up to Archie and Mary's home site. It was Archie's intention to build a stone tower on the remains of a subsurface structure that had been discovered, but when work started on this project some rather interesting things started to appear. Instead of just removing earth down to the level of the circular substructure, it was decided that a larger kiva discovered nearby should be more fully explored. This kiva was at least twenty feet in diameter, and had circular stone walls that were very carefully and solidly built. It was an impressive effort that led to a belief that it might have been an important ceremonial kiva in its time.

A number of room blocks surrounded the large kiva and Jerry and his crew were also in the process of digging in this area. There was no particular deadline in completing this project so Jerry and his crew came to work on our site during the period we were there to help. The following week, the crew would return to the Hanson site and continue working on it.

We decided to get to work on the ten square meter section of our kiva. Because we had found human remains in the southern end we were cautioned to work slowly in this area in which we were now digging. Most of what we had found so far were fairly small human bones but it was likely we would encounter larger pieces as we went along.

Both Diane and Kay worked in this section and I decided to dig in the opposite end. Since their work would proceed slowly, I was anxious to determine if we were getting close to the floor of the kiva. We were already down about four and half feet, and the bench sat up about three feet from where I was working. If any intact artifacts were to be found, they were most likely to be located on or near the kiva's floor. The previous day's finds acted as an incentive for me to locate more, and I quickly got to work.

Each screening of material produced a few more pottery sherds, the usual small flakes of lithic material, and even a few more small bones which would be examined further to determine if they were part of the skeletal remains already uncovered. No large human bones like a pelvis, skull, ribs, or vertebrae had yet been found. More and more charcoal was appearing in the area I was working on and some of the pieces were large enough to consider for further dendro analysis. In addition, near the center of the kiva, a few large stones were found which might indicate we had located the kiva's fire pit. But the stones were scattered and a clear pattern was not yet obvious.

Kay was busy making field notes of our morning's activities, and Diane took a break to run into town for a few supplies. Kelly was busy working in her trench and had discovered a rather large charred piece of wood opposite the one she had found yesterday. The more she worked, the more her materials indicated they were part of an upright support structure. Many times in an abandonment entire structures were burned by their former occupants perhaps for some ceremonial reason. On the other hand, it was equally likely that this structure might have been accidentally set on fire. Working around open fires was common and accidents were likely to occur. Whatever Kelly was finding, her work went along quite nicely but a bit slowly.

I cleaned up the section I had been digging and was somewhat disappointed to find that I had not yet reached the kiva floor. It was down there somewhere, but it must have been further down than any of us expected. When Jerry returned I was going to ask if it might be a good idea to take a core sample in the area just finished to help determine how far down the floor might be. But Jerry had not yet surfaced this morning; so I decided to dig in another section closer to where Diane and Kay had been working.

About a half-hour later I struck something with my patiche. At first I thought it might be a good-sized root because there were several that raced back and forth throughout the kiva. I stopped and dug around this obstruction with my fingers. I removed more and more dirt and the object came into sharper focus. It was a long and slender object over a foot long with a knob-like feature at either end. I wasn't certain what it might be and asked Kay to come take a look.

"I'm almost sure it's a femur bone," Kay said. "Let me take a look."

She climbed into the hole and brushed away more of the material surrounding the object. Within a few minutes we picked up a well preserved and intact human femur bone. "It's more of Pat, for sure." Kay said. "Let's take some shots and get the coordinates." She jumped out of the hole and had me help her with the survey.

As she worked behind the transit and prepared to take some more measurements, I asked about the location of this particular bone in relationship to the ones that had already been found. The femur is the large bone that runs from the pelvis to the knee in the upper portion of the human leg. Sometimes it's possible to estimate the height of an unknown person by measuring the length of this particular bone. Ours was quite long suggesting that its owner was quite tall—perhaps over six feet in height. I rested the bone against my own dirt covered leg just to check.

"Do you think it's from a male," I asked, "because of its length?"

"Could be, but the length isn't in itself conclusive," Kay replied. "If there's more of Pat here, we should be able to answer that question later. Then again, these bones might not be from just one individual. It's possible there were multiple burials here."

It's very likely we will never know who Pat was, or how or why his or her remains managed to get here. Death and burials had a wide range of practical and important ceremonial purposes for these early people. During periods when the weather was mild and a family member died, preparations were made quickly for burial. The body would be bathed and the deceased's hair thoroughly washed. Depending on the nature of the burial, the arms of the person were folded across the chest and often tied together to help them maintain a fetal-like position. When the legs were folded into position the tightly flexed body was then wrapped in a cotton blanket and sometimes even a second and larger feather blanket was wrapped around the body. Once this was completed, the bundle was wrapped in matting and the burial could begin.

There was no central place where the deceased were laid to rest. A burial could be made nearly anywhere. In good weather, a body might be laid out on a mesa top, or simply placed somewhere in one of the many canyons. Crevices in cliffs or even holes under large rock outcroppings served as a final resting place for many. In the winter, graves were often dug in trash piles found in front of each of the villages. If the weather was particularly bad, the family would sometimes just seal the body in an unused room, or even in an abandoned house. An indoor burial required that the body be surrounded by perfectly dry materials like ashes, corn cobs, corn tassels or even turkey droppings. The cold temperatures would keep the body from decaying, and the very dry winds in this area would allow the bones and tissue to remain without decomposing. This process produces a mummy-like condition that can allow the body to remain nearly unchanged for centuries.

Depending on the rank or status of the individual who died, a simple grave was usually dug in which the tightly-wrapped body was placed. Oftentimes the person was given objects to take with him into the next world. Food and water were placed in the grave along with important personal possessions like weapons, jewelry, tools, or other useful things that the deceased would need in the afterworld.

Again, depending on the time of the year and the circumstances of the burial, all remaining family members returned to their homes after the burial and began a process of self-purification. This consisted of washing themselves, particularly their hair, and was often followed by self-inflicted vomiting and fumigating their clothing in smoke.

Four days had to pass for the spirit of the deceased to leave the body. On each of the four mornings, relatives of the dead brought food and water to the grave site. Early in the morning of the fourth day, the person's spirit left the body and made a journey through the sipapu back into Mother Earth. Once there, the person's life went on much the same as the one they left. After the four days, all living relatives continued to purify themselves but their grieving had to end quickly. Grieving could cause sickness and it was best that the dead are quickly forgotten.

The human remains we were dealing with in our excavation seem to have been dumped into the kiva for no apparent reason. A pattern was emerging because the finger bones we discovered earlier were found close together in one general area. The femur was found in a line that ran from northeast to southwest. We had not yet found any rib bones, and the skull was likely to be found, if there was one, in the unexcavated portion of the trench.

There was one slightly curious feature on the femur bone. About a third of the way down, on the ankle end, a small growth was evident. It might be that the person's body tried to heal itself from some prior trauma. If more of this skeleton could be found, and a more complete forensic examination could be made, one might be able to piece together a more complete story about how long this person had lived, and we might even be able to gain some general idea about the person's overall health during life. But we had not yet discovered enough material to allow us to make a complete record about this person and his or her life. It was interesting, however, to discover that a great deal of information about an individual's life can be determined from rather incomplete physical evidence.

Just before our regular noon break, Jerry came back to the site. He seemed to be in his normal high spirits. As we all sat down to start eating our lunches, we brought him up to date on what we had been doing that morning.

With the exchange of information completed, we sat under our favorite shade tree and Jerry started to tell us about his rather interesting morning activities.

It started out with his checking up to see how Edmund was getting along. It seems as though he was making some progress at healing but his hand was still quite sore and painful. Edmund has been given some kind of pain killers by the doctors although Jerry didn't know if Edmund allowed himself to engage in such modern medical assistance. In any event, the man seemed to be getting along all right. It was his companion Cecil who had not fully recovered from his recent experience. It seems as though Cecil spent a rather restless night and Jerry relished recounting his story.

For some reason, Cecil needed to be up early that morning so rather than drive himself home last evening, he decided to spend the night not far from where he and Edmund had been working at the rock quarry. This particular area was on one of the Indian Camp Ranch residential lots that belonged to Archie Hanson's son. Archie's son was planning to build a second home on his lot and had come down with his family to camp for a few days to get a feel of things. Near the rock quarry, a small shelter of some kind had been found which provided a good place to camp. Archie's son was a wildlife devotee and found this location ideally suited for observing a wide area. It was near this site that Cecil spent the previous evening, and according to his story he spent a very restless night.

The larger archaeological features on each lot are identified by a three-inch metal pole that sticks up about ten feet in the air. About halfway down, a metal flange was welded which has a hinged top and flat base. By opening it, one can read a written description of the individual site, its features, and other general information that is written and housed under a thin sleeve of plastic. The data were taken from a larger archaeological survey that Jerry had made for Archie when the subdivision was first being planned. It helped potential property owners know a bit more about the features on their property, and it was interesting to observe these poles sticking up in no particular order and rising here and there as you drove around the subdivision. A hundred or more of these tall poles are scattered all over the place.

At the very top of each metal pole, Archie fashioned a metal cutout of Kokopelli—the famous southwestern fluteplayer whose figure can be found on all kinds of materials including tee-shirts and even jewelry. The graphic has been fashioned from some of the petroglyphs and pictographs which show the Kokopelli figure throughout the region. These shiny metal poles, with their Kokopelli tops, produced a wonderfully interesting contrast to the otherwise featureless land.

The previous night, just as Cecil tried to get to sleep, he claimed that all of the Kokopelli figures came to life. He watched as they gathered around the place where he tried to sleep. As more and more of the figures jumped off their poles they continued to dance around him and some of the figures became very bright. In fact, Cecil claimed that they took on a neon-like intensity and their colors were constantly changing, becoming bright red; then green; then orange. At the same time that the Kokopelli figures started to dance, Cecil was overcome with a terribly bloody nose. It wasn't just an everyday nosebleed, but one that couldn't be stopped. As the Kokopelli figures continued to dance and encircle him, Cecil became frightened and had to leave the area.

According to Cecil, his bloody nose could not be controlled and it wasn't until early in the morning that his wife found a medicine man who gave her some medicinal herbs that had to be administered by stuffing them up Cecil's nose. Within a short time, the bleeding stopped. It was a rather long and frightening night, and Cecil was taking the day off to recover from his ordeal.

We all enjoyed hearing Jerry's latest report. It seemed as though each day brought us another interesting tale of contemporary life as led by the interesting people of the Four Corners area.

Our afternoon activities consisted of taking down another ten-centimeter level of dirt in the southern end of the kiva. Toward the end of the day, we found a few additional human bones. Kay identified them as belonging to the foot. They were located in the northeastern portion of the site, again in a direct line with the femur and below the small bones of the hand. It was becoming more obvious that a single skeleton was most likely what we were uncovering although we had opened only half of the kiva structure and had no idea what additional remains might be found in the other section.

Diane and I had set aside just a week to participate in our project. We were well into our fourth day, and our trip was quickly coming to an end. My primary objective was to open one section of the site and see what could be found before making a decision to do further work in the following seasons. If we weren't uncovering much of interest, I wanted to make some test trenches in another one of the sites that was about 75 meters further south. This other site had a number of rather interesting and prominent surface features, suggesting a series of multi-storied room blocks could be unearthed along with a much larger kiva directly in front. There was some evidence of a plaza area, and perhaps even the foundation of a multi-storied tower. This project would be much more extensive than the one we were currently working on, and it would probably require several years of active digging.

Since it appeared that we were getting closer and closer to the floor of this kiva, we had a late afternoon meeting to discuss our plans for our remaining two days. We decided that we'd try to go down another ten centimeters across the entire structure to see if we could find the floor. Then we'd prepare to close the site for the year and decide later on what our work program would be for the next season.

Our day ended with showers and a wonderfully relaxing dinner with Jerry, his wife Linda Honeycutt, and their delightful six-year-old daughter Bonnie. Jerry took us out on his property to a place he called sunset rock. There, we watched a typically beautiful summer sunset that retained an orange glow in the sky for quite some time.

Tomorrow, the process would begin again.

CHAPTER eight

At first, Hosta thought he might never walk again.

Even now, after nearly a month recovering from the accident, he plays the events over and over again in his mind—particularly at night. The only things he can recall clearly are his hunting companions standing over him shouting his name over and over again. Then there are flashes of memory which recall the tremendous pain he suffered on a long journey back to his village.

As his memory slowly improves, Hosta remembers asking about the fawn and about the success of his hunting companions. Things are coming into better focus now and he seems to be feeling more like himself day-by-day. Hosta knows how fortunate he was, having Ika and an extra hand around. Tokana was able to provide valuable assistance by immediately running back to the village for help.

Ika immediately attended to Hosta's broken leg. Thin splints of wood were bound to his right leg so that the fractured bone could be set and given a chance to heal. When several men from the village arrived, they assisted in bringing Hosta back home where he receives as much attention as anyone could possibly hope for. Say makes a comfortable place for him to rest on the floor of their home and gathers a number of special healing herbs from which she makes a refreshing tea. Katti and her family arrive immediately upon learning of the hunting accident. Just as quickly, Tye summons one of the medicine men to attend to the injury. Accidents of all kinds happen quite frequently and many of the injuries can ultimately prove fatal. It is most likely that a single fracture will heal if properly treated and if the medicine men are skillful in performing their rituals and ceremonies. Compound fractures, however, are not as easily treated as oftentimes infections occur and result in much suffering before death takes away the pain. The worst kind of fracture is to the head, and fortunately these kinds of accidents do not occur frequently.

Hosta has suffered a fracture and there is usually some form of permanent damage when a limb is fractured, although healing depends greatly on the severity of the problem and the care given. Any fracture of the upper arm or leg, such as the one Hosta has suffered, is seldom treated with complete success. The muscles cause the healing bones to be pulled out of position and if no other medical complications occur, and some crippling is the usual result. It is too early to tell if Hosta will suffer any long-term disability because of his accident although everyone is relieved that his bad fever has passed.

A day after being brought back to the village, Hosta develops an infection and an unusually high fever. The first medicine man is brought in to perform his usual routine of praying and preparing and administering various medicines. On the first evening the medicine man also smears ashes all over his hands to protect him from the witches. He then performs a complete physical examination of Hosta, although it Is quite obvious what the ultimate diagnosis will be. The medicine man makes certain adjustments to the splint on

Hosta's entire right leg, and then mixes a number of powdered herbs together with water and gives this potion to
Hosta to drink. It tastes terrible and Hosta nearly spits out
most of it before being encouraged to make sure he con-
sumes every last drop. But not even this extreme amount of
care seems to help much, as Hosta spends a very restless
night during which he develops an extremely high fever.

The next morning Tye decides that something more
needed to be done for his nephew than a single medicine
man could provide. Mixing a small amount of corn meal
with some powdered turquoise and wrapping it in a corn
husk, Tye plans to take this offering to one of his friends
who is a member of the medicine society. This simple offering is a request for a more involved healing ceremony and
it suggests a deepening concern both he and his sister are
having for this rather sick young man.

"I should leave right now," Tye says, "and you should
continue keeping him as comfortable as possible. Keep his
forehead cool with water and make sure that he drinks the
medicines. I'll be back before nightfall."

"Thank you brother," Say responds. "He sleeps so fit-
fully that I am not sure he is getting any rest at all."

As Tye and Say walk with each other down the path,
young Katti comes toward them carrying something with
her in a small jar.

"How is he?" Katti asks. The eyes of her soon-to-be relatives convey the message.

"He has fever now, and Tye is on his way to summon the
medicine society," Say responds.

Katti's heart races as she knows what this means. He is
not getting better, and more efforts will be needed to heal
Hosta and make him well again.

"I will go and sit with him for as long as it takes for him
to recover," Katti responds and runs the rest of the way
down the path, and rushes inside the house.

Extensive preparations will need to be made by all of
Hosta's family, and the women will need to make great

quantities of food for the members of the medicine society who come to their village to provide assistance. Everyone will need to cleanse themselves completely, as they know that the next four days will require their intense involvement if the healing process is to be successful.

Normally a sick person needs to be taken to the kiva of the medicine society where the various rituals are performed. In Hosta's case, he is much too ill to be taken anywhere, and his own home will have to serve for the purpose.

That evening five of the most powerful medicine men come to help Hosta with his recovery. Two of the men station themselves outside the house armed with bows and arrows. They are there to ensure that no witches enter the place where the sick person is. Inside, three of the medicine men began smoothing out a place on the floor of the house. As this is done, several prayer sticks are placed around where Hosta is lying on the ground. One of the medicine men brings a bag of several different items and is busy placing them all around inside the house. Several carved stones, some in the shape of various animals, are placed around the smooth place that has been made on the floor.

Each doctor comes with his face heavily painted and is dressed simply in a loincloth. Each carries several bags of finely-powdered cornmeal, which they now start to open as they begin their chants. Their singing is an attempt to summon the spirits of the healing animals like the mountain lion, bear, badger, wolf, and eagle. Everyone knows that these particular animals have tremendous supernatural healing powers and their spirits must be aroused and brought into the house for the healing ceremonies to be successful.

Hosta, Katti, and the entire family watch these preparations carefully. Katti keeps wiping Hosta's forehead with cool water using a soft piece of deerskin. From time to time Hosta shivers a little which indicates that the fever has still not gone from his body. He looks around the room noting the seriousness of everyone present. He knows that he is in pain, and that whatever is happening to him is completely in the hands of these men from the medicine society and the gods. Hosta sighs deeply just before the next part of the ceremony is about to begin.

Two of the medicine men open their bags of powdered cornmeal and begin making a small painting on the ground they had made smooth. As they hold the cornmeal between their thumbs and forefingers, they sing and chant and drop the colored meal in an exact pattern on the ground. Everyone in the room remains silent and very still as this process goes on for quite a long time. When they finish, they place several more prayer sticks and fetish carvings around the completed painting. Even a few eagle feathers are used to brush the dusty cornmeal into the exact positions required.

A few more herbs are mixed with water and the chanting and signing continues for what seemed like hours. It is now the middle of the night and Hosta's grandmother has fallen asleep where she is sitting. Say, however, remains alert and watches everything with great intensity. Unfortunately, she has been through this before. These ceremonies are not unlike those she has witnessed many times before and she remains concerned because not all these ceremonial activities have proven entirely successful in the past. Several years ago, before she married, two of her own family members did not live to see the new morning and she can not keep these negative thoughts from her mind.

Hosta himself has fallen into a fitful sleep. Katti is nearly asleep but continues to listen to the whispering of the prayers of the medicine men and keeps her vigil throughout the long night.

As the first light of the new day emerges, the medicine men finish their chants and prayers and get up to walk outside the house. As part of the cleansing they must do, yet another bag of herbs is opened and mixed with water. Each of the medicine men takes a drink from the cup that is then passed around to everyone who has attended the healing ceremony. Within a few minutes they each vomit, which is the intended and required result of the process. The strong herbs which have been mixed together act as an emetic and yet for some of the ceremony participants it does not induce vomiting. When this happens, one of the medicine men will take a long feather and thrust it down the person's throat until the intended result is obtained.

Depending on the nature and severity of the illness being cured, the ceremony usually goes on for four days. If this time passes and there is no improvement, the family is given whatever comfort there is and the medicine men return to their own villages where everyone must just hope for the best. Oftentimes this is all that can be done and if the witches have become too powerful, death will be the ultimate result.

On the fourth morning of the ceremony, Hosta awakens and becomes fully aware of the people and events around him. His mind is much clearer, and his terrible shaking of the past few days seems to have gone away. Katti is the first to notice the change.

"Hosta, how are you feeling this morning?" she asks.

"I am feeling much better, but the pain in my leg is still there especially when I try to move into a more comfortable position," he responds.

Tye observes this conversation and comes over to kneel before his nephew.

"How you doing?" he asks.

"I think much better," is the reply.

And so it was that on the morning of the fourth day, Hosta's fever lifts and he begins a slow recovery. Among the family there are expressions of gratitude to the medicine men and several baskets of cornmeal are given to them in exchange for their successful efforts. The women cleanse themselves then begin preparing a great feast. Everyone celebrates their cautious elation that Hosta seems to be making a recovery from the accident and illness he has suffered.

The hunting trip itself wasn't entirely unsuccessful. Even while he was in excruciating pain, Hosta had managed to strangle and kill one of the fawns and his two hunting companions were also successful in tracking down and killing another. Ika and Tokana did an excellent job in removing the precious hide and split up the meat among each of their families, including Hosta's. And because they both knew what Hosta had intended to do with these valuable hides, they gave them to one of the trading parties that left their village for a trip to the south. Within a few days they hoped that enough white cotton would be returned so that Hosta could decide what to do about the blanket he wants to weave for his bride-to-be.

Hosta's healing process continues, and later in the summer Hosta feels his strength returning. He even manages to take a few very awkward and painful steps using a wooden cane that his uncle has made for him. To help Hosta gain back his strength, Say has prepared some green corn stew using the deer meat along with some of the first tender ears of corn from the season's crop. This green corn comes from the plants whose ears are not fully developed but have a soft, tender, and milky kernel. These still-maturing ears are a delicacy for the people who roast, bake, or boil, and consume great quantities of them. Some of the green corn is prepared for winter use and it is also roasted and ground into a fine meal which is carefully stored away. During the darkest and coldest times of winter it will be made into a delicious mush and mixed with hot water to produce a very welcome hot drink.

In the later part of August, just before the nights began to take on more and more of a chill, the Town Crier stood on the roof of his home and announced that the annual green corn festival would be held in two days' time. With that announcement, all people in the many villages and settlements of the area started to prepare for the feasting and celebrating which would soon take place.

Everyone who is physically able rushes to the fields on the morning of the appointed day. The day after the Crier Chief makes his announcement, the men start to dig deep pits near the fields and gather huge amounts of firewood. One night before the festival, fires are started in the pits and all throughout the night the men and boys continue placing huge amounts of fuel on the fires. They also gamble, tell stories of the summer that is now quickly coming to a close, and wait for the celebrating they will begin in the morning.

Soon after the sun rises, the green corn stalks and leaves are being picked by everyone from each of the villages, and as the fires die out, ashes are being scraped away. Then the green stalks and leaves are used to line each pit. Hundreds of ears of freshly-picked corn, tightly wrapped in their still-growing husks, are tossed into the pits. When a mound of corn is formed, the dirt that was dug to create the pit is tossed on top and sealed. Throughout the day the corn will steam in these huge earthen ovens.

It is a day of celebration and one that Hosta knows he cannot miss. Although his strength is not what it had been before the accident he is helped by Katti, Ika, and several members of the family and hobbles out into the fields where he is greeted by nearly every member of the village who offers him their best wishes and hopes for a full recovery.

Several small fires are being built around the edges of the fields and many of the women and girls are busily engaged in preparing a wide variety of dishes that will be consumed later. The men continue to gossip, trade, and gamble. The youngsters romp about the fields and started challenging each other in a variety of running games and other contests. The younger men and boys set up targets and use bow and arrows to try their skill to see who might be the most accurate and, perhaps one day, the best hunter. The day is sunny and mild, and what appears to be an excellent crop is praised by the women. Many thanks are given to the priests and the chiefs who successfully helped contribute to the season's bounty.

As the day passes and a cool breeze kicks up from the west to make the corn leaves rustle, the actual feast begins. The farmers open their pits and the hot, steaming, tender ears of green corn are quickly passed around to everyone present. This is one of the great events of the year and one that is cherished by all people of the villages. Their great celebration continues all throughout the evening. Everyone is elated by the fine crops, the good cheer, and harmony that is very much in evidence throughout the day.

After taking their fill of green corn and many other good things to eat, Katti and Hosta quietly drift away from the noisy celebration to find a place where they can talk together.

"You are getting around nicely," Katti says as she holds on to Hosta's left arm.

"Yah, I really think this stupid leg of mine might be all right after all," is his reply. "Still don't know how I managed to trip over that rock in the first place."

"Why were you out hunting anyway?" Katti asks. "And why didn't the others go with you?"

"It was for a special reason," Hosta replies. "And it sorta involves you.."

"Me? What are you talking about?"

"Can't tell you right now. It's a surprise that you'll know about one of these days soon enough."

The two continue talking about a variety of things for several hours. They express their growing love and affection for one other. The evening's breeze picks up and is now beginning to blow out of the north. The slight chill in the air changes to being much cooler and they soon decide to return to the physical warmth of the many fires that will continue to burn throughout the night. There is no doubt about it, fall is in the air and even that season will quickly pass into winter.

Hosta's recovery continues throughout the late summer and into early fall. He is not yet strong enough to consider joining the men in planning their annual hunting trips, and spends much of his time working on the cotton blanket he is preparing as a gift for Katti.

More than enough pure white cotton was brought to him by the trading party returning from the south. Because the skins of the spotted fawns had been so well received in the southern villages, an extra special item had been negotiated and traded for and brought back for Hosta. A huge sea shell, quite unlike those that many had ever been seen before, was given to him. The shell would be greatly admired by everyone and could be very useful in making some very special jewelry.

What the people of Hosta's village lack in the way of clothing, they make up for in jewelry. Both men and women wear necklaces, pendants, and earrings made from a variety of exotic materials. Precious turquoise is becoming more and more common among the items of adornment, but every now and then shell is brought back by various trading parties. Necklace beads are made from these shells, from bones, and particularly from seeds which have always been very popular. The large sea shell which Hosta was given in partial exchange for the spotted fawn skins will not only be greatly admired, but very useful in the making of jewelry. It could also be easily used to trade for other useful things he and his new bride might need.

With the assistance of some of the older men of his village, Hosta is shown how to make and prepare a weaving loom and is also shown how to prepare raw cotton for weaving. Weaving is primarily a winter activity of the men who mostly do their work in their kivas. All of the older men are more than happy to share their knowledge and talents with Hosta. Only a few of the younger men seem interested in keeping the art of weaving alive, so when Hosta announced his intentions of weaving a cotton blanket, nearly every one of the older men had offered him his help and assistance.

The loom itself is a simple device consisting of two upright poles, and two horizontal poles which are then warped so that actual weaving can begin. The loom on which Hosta will weave his blanket is set up in one of his relative's houses so that Katti and others will not know about this secret project. Because Hosta is still unable to do much active physical work, he quickly takes to this new task and spends many hours each day preparing his cotton under the watchful and helpful eyes of the elder men. The repetitive nature of the work is quite relaxing and helps the days pass quickly.

The light of each new day is growing shorter and shorter. The first frosts of October bring rich color to the mesas to the south. Some of the scrub oak and other ground covers are beginning to alight in a blaze of color. Everyone in each of the villages is up early to help bring in the final harvest of the growing season. Dozens of baskets are carried into the fields where squash and beans and corn are gathered and brought home for processing and storage.

Some of the corn is husked right in the fields and then taken home. At times the corn stalks are cut at ground level and the entire plant is taken home where leaves, tassels, and shucks are used in a variety of ways. The bean crop is usually dried in the fields and after drying the women come back with sticks and beat them until the beans are freed from their pods. Pods and beans are then placed in baskets that are tossed lightly to separate the beans from the pods and any other foreign debris.

Squashes grow in many sizes and colors. They are all used and prepared in a variety of ways. Some of the larger squashes are quite heavy and it takes hours of work to pick and carry the heaviest of them back to the village. Everyone is involved in the harvest. Youngsters, their parents and grandparents all participate in the many harvesting activities of fall.

Along with the parade of color from the surrounding foliage, each of the villages becomes an explosion of color as well. Nearly the entire harvest is spread out to dry on the roofs or is scattered in the courtyards to the point that simply moving around is sometimes difficult. Corn is grown in many varieties, some of which produces bright red kernels. Others are blue, or black, or white.

From morning until all light of day is gone, activities continue. The proper storage of food supplies is always the responsibility of the women. Men are responsible for planting and growing the crops and they participate in the harvest, but once the harvest is over it is the women who again take charge. The women in each household will store their foodstuffs together and at times they will give away much of their harvest to the older families of the village or to those who might not otherwise have enough food to see them through the long winter to come.

Although some of the corn is shelled immediately, and some used for each of the evening meals, most of it will be stored on the cob. The corn is separated into colors and the bright ears are stacked like cordwood in the houses or in the many storage rooms around the villages. Beans are stored in baskets and pottery jars but the squash can be stored almost anywhere. Many of the squashes are peeled and then cut into long strips. After these strips have dried, they are rolled up in bundles and then put away in one of the storage rooms. During the winter they will be soaked in water that actually restores their flavor. Squash is a welcome addition to an otherwise drab winter day.

The storage of food is vital to these people. Because every one of the older people of the village has lived through drought and poor growing seasons, they prepare at least a three-year supply of food to be available should something happen. They also know how important it is to seal the storage areas from any intrusion by animals like rodents, and how dampness will rot the food if it is not properly prepared. Corn tassels are often used to protect grains from dampness.

The finest looking ears of corn will be set aside separately and carefully protected, as these ears will become the source of the seed for next season's planting and for various ceremonial purposes as well. The farmers are gifted at deciding which of the ears of corn are the best and will most likely produce the most abundant crops in the future. They too are separated from each other by color and extra care is taken to protect these ears from either dampness or from varmints. Pottery jars are often used to store the seed corn although many people continue to leave the corn on the cob and not remove it until the next planting season actually begins.

In addition to harvesting their own crops, the fall is a busy time for the collection of other important agricultural products. The women scour the mesas and canyons for many valuable products. One of their favorite items is pinyon nuts. Early frosts will open the seed-bearing cones of the pinyon trees and the ground will be covered with these brown nuts which are just a bit smaller than the beans the people grow. A great contest results as the people compete with squirrels and chipmunks for the prized pinyon nuts. There are many seasons when the pinyon nuts are plentiful and others when the people need to travel several miles in order to gather enough of the nuts for their winter needs. Then there are times when pinyon nuts are not produced at all, which is a bad sign to the people. For many, it reminds them of how important it is to store food and prepare for the times that will not be as abundant as this season has been.

Besides pinyon nuts, there are many other plants that the women gather and store for winter. They include yucca pods, cactus fruits, berries, and roots and seeds of all kinds. A number of medicinal herbs that have grown throughout the summer are now ready to be gathered and dried. All during the fall and winter each of the houses will have many drying plants hung on the walls.

Fall is also the important hunting season for the men. Several hunts are organized by the Hunt Chief and the women will soon take time away from gathering and storage of crops for the difficult task of skinning deer, elk, and mountain goat. The fall is a very busy time and as each of the days grows shorter, everyone becomes increasingly aware of the winter season coming upon them.

Winter is not a good time for the people. The witches are very active in the winter and many of the people will suffer greatly. If it is particularly cold for long periods of time, or if snows are not abundant, long trips will need to be made to the springs where water must be obtained and brought home. It is the older people who will suffer the most during the winter and many of them may not live through the season if it is harsh or if they become sick and weakened.

Hosta and his family have spent a great deal of time preparing for the coming winter. More than enough food has been stored to last this and several seasons to come. The turkeys have feasted on corn and are now fat. The people of Hosta's village have added a few extra pounds of weight for the coming winter season. Hosta's strength is improving and each day he is able to put more and more weight on his right leg. Things seem to be healing quite nicely and he even engages in a few exercises to help limber up his muscles that have become weak from so little use. Both his physical and mental confidence are increasing and the frequent visits from Katti help to energize him even more.

How lucky he is to be enjoying life and how optimistic he has become in considering his future. Hosta gains confidence that this leg will heal completely, and that the season has been a good one for the crops, and he looks forward to being the husband of his lovely young Katti.

Life is sweet and to be enjoyed, but it is uncertain as well.

CHAPTER
nine

The last full day of work on our project was rather uneventful.

The discovery of human remains had slowed our digging activities and a number of other factors caused us to slow our pace. We had not yet reached the kiva floor although we suspected we were getting very close. Diane and I had a number of obligations awaiting us back home and we needed to stick with our original schedule of returning our motor home to Durango so we were not able to add any more days to our current schedule. However, we wanted to be around when the digging would reveal the floor and didn't want Jerry and the crew to finish the work without us. So we decided on a plan that included a number of things.

First, we would arrange to come back and work with the crew for a few more days in the fall when I needed to come down for the annual meeting of the Crow Canyon Archaeological Center. We would plan to work as long as it would take to reach the kiva floor. We also decided to prepare the site for winter by building a wood and plastic cover and agreed to decide later if we would schedule the next season and continue work on this project or perhaps move on to the larger site.

We finished our work that day and were all quite satisfied with what we had accomplished during the week. We would be back in a few months to pick up where we had left off, and the long months of winter would be used to analyze many of the materials we had found. Jerry, Kelly, and Kay would begin working to prepare the written reports on our site. Diane and I were excited that we would be able to return in the fall and finish the project we had come here to be involved in.

We returned in early October just in time to witness the splendid display of fall colors that seem to be much more intense and vivid in the special sunlight of the Southwest. The days were sunny and bright but it was certainly much cooler. Shorts and tee-shirts were no longer the uniform of the day.

During the first week of October, we quickly uncovered the kiva and got to work. The first order of business was to drill three test holes at the bottom of the excavation to determine how far down that elusive floor might be. Jerry dug the holes with his trusty hand auger and analyzed the samples as he went along. It wasn't long before he discovered that what appeared to be compacted dirt was a mere 20 cm down. This compacted earth was clear evidence that the floor was close at hand and it was certain that we could complete our project within the two days we had allotted.

We got to work and brought each other up to date on the many things that had transpired since we were last together. The team went back to work on Archie Hanson's site after we left and were discovering a variety of interesting artifacts as they went along.

One exciting piece of news was that the first home to be built at the Indian Camp Ranch had been completed just a few weeks ago. The house was built by a wonderfully energetic and extremely personable lady by the name of Nancy Reynolds. She had most recently been involved in national politics in Washington, D.C. and was the head of her own prestigious and successful lobbying organization. She had recently given up her life's work there and was now living in Santa Fe. Nancy was also a very active and important contributing volunteer to Crow Canyon, and like most of the other property owners at Indian Camp Ranch, she was anxious to spend as much time as she could in this fascinating area and was the first property owner to proceed with building her second home.

Nancy chose to build a modified log home on her property. The site she selected sits on a high ridge and provides a spectacular and unobstructed view in all directions. One of the best features of her home is a covered porch that nearly surrounds her home and offers a distinctive and inviting amenity.

Building anything in this area of the country provides a kaleidoscope of opportunities, frustrations, and challenges. There aren't many regulatory obstructions or delays that are getting to be more and more common in other parts of the civilized West. But there is a variety of cultural and logistical impediments that are equally challenging.

Work crews often have their own ideas about deadlines. Time is not a particularly critical commodity in this area of the world, and getting things done on a schedule is often an unnecessary intrusion into the way things normally are accomplished. Nancy was trying to complete her project against a deadline for a variety of reasons, not the least of which was an invitation to have her new home featured in an upcoming issue of Mary Emmerling's *Style Magazine*. To meet the publication deadline, her home needed to be completed and all furnishings in place within a prescribed period of time. Because the concept of setting goals and meeting deadlines is a lost art in this region of the world, her building project was far from on schedule. But the house did eventually get finished and it is a lovely and inviting place that Nancy and her many friends will be sure to enjoy for years to come.

In celebrating the completion of her home Nancy wondered if she might have the honor of having her home blessed. Some time before his accident, Cecil had volunteered information that one of his relatives had performed many house blessings for people on and off the Navajo reservation and would be more than happy to assist in seeing that this important honor was bestowed on Nancy's beautiful new home.

Jerry told us about the proposed house blessing while we made plans for our last day of activity at the site. None of us had ever witnessed a house blessing before and we were excited for Nancy and agreed that it would be a great honor to witness one.

A little before noon on our next-to-last-day of work, Nancy drove up to our site. She inquired about the progress of our activities and then kindly invited us all to join in the celebration of her house blessing. We were all excited about being invited. She went on to explain some of the details that were scheduled to begin that evening.

First, we were to arrive at her home just before sunset. The house blessing would take place as the sun started to set in the west. Once we were in the house, and the blessing began, no one would be able to leave until the entire ceremony was over. We inquired about how long this whole process might take, but no one had provided her any information on the details; so we were to show up and it would take however long it took.

Nancy had been given some other instructions about various things that would be needed for the house blessing and so was quickly off town in order to do some shopping for the necessary items. Just after she drove off to town, we all made plans to finish up our day's work early enough to get cleaned up and arrive in plenty of time for the festivities that evening. We were all quite pleased that

Nancy had invited us to join her. Our daily activities went along smoothly and without incident.

Later that afternoon Nancy drove back to inform us that she had been in contact with Cecil once again who explained that he had managed to get a few things all messed up. His relatives who were to perform the ceremony had reminded him that a house blessing had to take place at the first light of a new day, not at sunset. Armed with this critical new piece of information our plans were quickly altered. We would all meet at Nancy's house very early in the morning.

Somewhere along the line it was also reported that one of the special requirements after a house blessing was to serve all the assembled guests and house blessers a feast of mutton stew. It wasn't a traditional breakfast item for most of us, but what the heck, we were honored to have an opportunity to participate in this important event. Kelly volunteered to provide the stew and she would need to leave a bit early so she could get to the store and pick up a few things in order to work that evening on preparing the dish.

The next morning, long before the sun would illuminate the day, our motel room phone rang. It seems there was some updated information that would require us to be at Nancy's home a bit earlier than we had anticipated. So we got up and got on our way.

We arrived at Nancy's house and were introduced to the other invited guests. Archie and Mary Hanson were in town and came by as excited about everything as all of us were. Then the contractor and some of the workmen who had been involved in building the house were there. Jerry arrived with his daughter, and one of Nancy's friends from California was there. Kelly arrived with a huge pot of mutton stew and it took everyone a few minutes to figure out how to use the new stove to keep the stew simmering for the celebration that would follow the house blessing.

The pale light of a new day emerged to the east, and no one had yet shown up other than our group of observers.

But we knew that the house blessers would certainly arrive shortly.

Coffee was ready and a huge bowl of goodies had been set out on a table. Someone had been informed that a proper beginning to the ceremony would be to have a variety of food available to be used as offerings. The bowl was appropriately filled with Snickers bars, Frito corn chips, mixed nuts, and other treats. No one was quite certain if these things would be considered acceptable to the house blessers, but the effort was greatly appreciated by many of us.

In addition to being told that offerings of food would be required before beginning the blessing, and that mutton stew would need to be served right after the blessing ceremony was over, Cecil told Nancy sometime yesterday that she should be prepared to cook up an ample supply of fry bread. Fry bread is the Navajo equivalent of eating raw fat in copious quantities. Some have described Indian fry bread as a warm and circular heart attack. But there is no one who will dispute that fry bread is a delicious delicacy which just can't be beaten when dipped into mutton stew or served as a dessert with huge quantities of honey.

Nancy had indicated to Cecil that she was well stocked up with flour and lard and all the essentials of fry bread making. But Cecil had made an inquiry about the kind of flour she had on hand. Nancy believed it was one of the usual brands of flour—perhaps it was one of the high altitude varieties because we were at about 7,000 feet which is where unusual culinary things happen if you don't provide for proper recipe adjustments.

"But you must use the special flour," was Cecil's reply.

"And where do I get that?" Nancy asked.

"At the City Market in Cortez of course," Cecil said.

And so in one of her many shopping trips into town Nancy went to search out the flour. She looked everywhere in the store and could not locate it. Finally she asked one of the clerks if they had that "special" flour, and sure enough, they did.

"But I can't find it on the shelf," Nancy said.

"Well that's because we keep it in back," the clerk responded with near incredulity.

"In back? Why do you keep it there?"

"'Cause it only comes in 50-pound bags and takes up far too much display space. But everyone knows we have it and where we keep it," the clerk observed.

Sitting just inside Nancy's pantry was a lifetime supply of fry bread flour that can be used at times of ceremonial blessings and other important feasts.

Nancy was wearing a beautiful buckskin dress for the occasion. She even had a pair of finely made moccasins and was in the process of putting on a pair of colorful beaded anklets that had been given to her by one of the Plains Indian tribes several years ago. She was having some difficulty getting them zipped up by herself so we suggested that she flop face down on her bed and we'd see if we couldn't provide some assistance. It took a while, but the job got done, although the photograph we took of her being helped into the anklets looks more like we were trying to shoe a horse. But Nancy is a great sport and took everything in stride.

It was getting a bit late, and some us were worried about whether or not Cecil really had all his facts straight and if he had somehow managed to miscommunicate the details again. Then someone remembered that Cecil and the house blessers probably lived on the Navajo reservation in Arizona, and Arizona is one of those strange places that doesn't participate in the unnatural practice of daylight savings time. It would have been an hour earlier on the reservation that perhaps could account for the tardy arrival of the group. Archie Hanson, being the persistent purveyor of logic, quickly reminded us all that the Navajos didn't subscribe to the arcane observance of time anyway and it was unlikely that this was the reason for the delay.

Someone else suggested we try to call Cecil to see what might be holding things up. But then we remembered that there are few phones on the Navajo reservation and it was not likely that Cecil, or any member of his family, might even have a phone. So we just decided to wait.

As much as we had a good time discussing the delightful nature of the Navajo people, we were certain they were having just as good of a time discussing the strange behavior of their white friends. In fact, the Navajo have a truly wonderful sense of humor and often delight in putting us on.

Kelly related a story of having attended the Navajo Nation's tribal fair that was held the previous Saturday down in Shiprock, New Mexico. She and her boyfriend had gone to the fair, and Diane and I also went down to take a look at things earlier the same day.

Community celebrations are wonderful to observe in any culture and the Navajo people are among the best at enjoying their community activities. Everyone comes to help decorate a float in the parade, march in the band, ride on one of the tribal fire trucks, or simply exchange stories and goodwill with each other. The kids all dress up, some of them in traditional dress, and the people smile warmly and greet us outsiders with much warmth and affection.

The main east-west road into Shiprock is Highway 64 that narrows to a two-lane bridge over the San Juan River. This is the only bridge across the river for miles in either direction, and the old highway and bridge to the south of the newer one served as the parade route through town. The bridge quickly fills up with cars, trucks, and thousands of pickups, and people have difficulty finding places to park along the parade route. A massive traffic jam is the result and even earlier in the morning, before the actual parade and festivities were to begin, Diane and I had a hard time getting to the west side of bridge to find a place to park from which we could walk through the exhibits at the fair grounds and shop for any intriguing craft items that are always found in great abundance at such events.

It didn't take us long to get a bit frustrated with not finding a place to park, and the lack of a finding a good variety of things to buy or eat. So we decided to get back on the road and drive back to our site where we could continue working on our project.

Getting out of town and back to the main highway became more of a challenge as the day wore on. We quickly determined that the only way we were going to find our way out of town was to drive west into Arizona, and then take Highway 160 north and cross the river. As it turned out, this was a good decision, even though it took us miles out of our way. We were told later on that after about noon getting across the bridge was nearly impossible, so we were glad we made the decision we had.

Kelly and her boyfriend arrived sometime later in the day and had the same difficulty finding a place to park and reaching the fairgrounds. They wisely elected to park on the east side of the bridge and walk over it to the fairgrounds. In doing so, they strolled behind a group of very young and energetic Navajo men and women who were having a wonderful time joking with each other and loudly greeting several friends along the way. According to Kelly, about halfway across the bridge the group stopped suddenly and asked if Kelly and her boyfriend would mind posing so that they could take their picture. Of course it was fine with them, but Kelly asked why in the world these young people wanted to have a picture of two strangers.

"We just don't see many white people on this bridge," one of them replied, "you are a great novelty to us."

At first Kelly was taken aback but when everyone in their group started to laugh in unison, and there didn't appear to be a camera anywhere in sight, they quickly caught on to the fact that these youngsters had very skillfully put them on. It was more than likely that each of them had been in situations where a white tourist would have asked any one of them if they minded posing for a picture while explaining that they just didn't run into many Native Americans where they came from.

Kelly also said that upon returning to their car later that day, they were walking behind a nicely dressed young

Navajo man. He seemed to be decked out in a pair of new boots, a rakish western hat, and a nicely made belt with a silver and turquoise buckle. Every now and then this fellow would jump up in the air and clap his heels together and let out a little "whoop." This went on for some time and after they had all crossed the bridge the young fellow again did a little dance, jumped and whooped, and then simply stood in place. As Kelly and her boyfriend passed him by, he was heard to say to no one in particular, "Sometimes I even surprise myself."

It was now about nine in the morning and nothing was happening. We all had a wonderful time discussing a wide variety of things, and everyone greatly admired the workmanship and quality of the house Nancy had built. Equally, many expressed some concern about Cecil and the house blessing party. No one dared utter what some of us had briefly thought to ourselves. The incidence of highway traffic accidents and even death is very high among the Navajo people, and some of the other Indian nations of the Southwest. Alcohol is very much a part of these accidents and tragic events, although there are certainly other factors that play a role in the rate and frequency of highway accidents. Many of the vehicles driven by the native people are older model cars and pickup trucks that are perhaps not as well maintained as they should be. These are not wealthy people who can afford new cars or trucks every few years, and they must live with what they have and attempt to keep up with whatever demands arise despite any obstacles placed before them. There is a variety of reasons for the high mortality rate among highway users, and we all quietly hoped that this was in no way responsible for the late arrival of the blessing crew.

Diane and I needed to be thinking about getting back home and it was getting late. We would need to get on the road no later than 9:30 if we were going to arrive in time for some of the obligations we had back home. We very reluctantly decided it was time to get on the road. The blessing crew didn't seem to be anywhere in sight, and we were very unhappy about having to leave. At the same time everyone in attendance had other things to do that day, and the unpleasant thought that something terrible might have happened to the blessing crew was unspoken.

We said our goodbyes to everyone, gave our own special blessing to Nancy's fine new home and then simply had to leave. We waved our farewell to those handsomely dressed women and hoped that everything would work out.

Several weeks later, after we arrived back home, we called to see how things were getting along. We heard some very interesting and at the same time some very distressing news.

The house blessing ceremony did take place. Within about a half-hour of our departure, the crew of house blessers arrived. There didn't seem to be any explanation as to why they had been delayed, and there probably wasn't much point in asking anyway. The whole concept of time and schedules is not something in the lexicon of the kindly and sometimes quirky ways of the Navajo people.

We were told that everyone assembled inside the house, and the chanting and the blessing ceremony began. We were told it took all of about ten minutes. And then the feasting began, and everyone had a great time. Nancy was delighted to have her house appropriately blessed and Cecil was proud that he once again had added to the happiness of these curious white people he had worked around for so long.

Then Kay told us about the discovery they had made in the kiva they were digging at Archie's site. As they dug deeper and deeper, they discovered a number of human remains as they got closer and closer to the kiva floor. But these bones were not in good condition. She reported that not one of them was more than about two inches in length and that they each had evidence of being brutally severed and broken. So far they had recovered the fractured remains of about five, perhaps six, different persons.

No one knew if the bones had been destroyed violently after the people had died of natural causes, or if they had been hacked into pieces and killed in some kind of ritual. Cannibalism was not unknown to these people and enemies were not treated kindly. But it was impossible to speculate on the fate of these people and their remains were being sent to an archaeological research organization for further analysis.

Kay indicated that at least one of the severed skeletons was that of a child. They also speculated that the remains were made up from two males and two females. How and why these remains managed to be buried in the kiva can only be speculated by us today. Perhaps some further research on the remains will provide clues to the mystery.

What all of this news meant to us is nothing more than reinforcing how little we really know about these fascinating prehistoric peoples. What little we do about how they lived and died is minuscule in comparison to what we don't know. And we may never be able to know everything we'd like to.

The art and science of archaeology will continue to provide us with much more valuable information and insight in the years to come. The sophistication of the tools to be used in this fascinating process of discovery will certainly increase dramatically. But long after every last artifact is located and catalogued, and every last fragment is fit into the puzzle that tells us more about our shared cultural history, we will still not know with any precision how these people lived, what they thought and believed, or how we might more fully understand their place on this shared planet of human activity and endeavor.

The mystery of their lives will remain to be solved and may quite possibly never be entirely clear.

epilogue

William the Conqueror is one of the primary figures in every textbook ever written on the history of western civilization. He was born at Falaise in the Normandy region of northwestern France. He could just as easily have been named "William the Bastard," because he was the illegitimate son of Robert I, the first Duke of Normandy, and Herleva, a tanner's daughter. At the age of eight, William's father died and William inherited all of present-day Normandy. It was a turbulent time although William and his followers managed to hold on to the inheritance with the able assistance of King Henry I of France. Over time, William grew to be a strong and forceful leader and a great soldier as well.

Troubles at home notwithstanding, William claimed that the English monarch, King Edward the Confessor, had promised him succession to the English throne because William claimed to be one of King Edward's nearest living relatives. It is true that Edward and Robert I were related, but it was Edward's brother Harold who saw things differently and declared himself to be the new King of England. Fortunately for him, the claim garnered the support of various English noblemen including the all-important local clergy. William was a man of great ambition and became angry and disappointed when he learned of this course of events. He then did what every proper-thinking empire builder would do at the time. He raised an army and decided to invade England in order to reclaim his rightful turf.

Fortunately for William, Harold was busy fighting off a bunch of Norwegian invaders who had crossed into northern England during the turmoil of deciding the English succession. While Harold was away on business, William and his army crossed the English Channel and promptly took control of the southern coast. William's troops destroyed Harold's Anglo-Saxon army and later killed Harold himself soon after he arrived to defend this latest invasion.

The spoils of war went to William the Conqueror who was crowned King of England in Westminster Abbey. He kept most of the lands he had conquered for himself but wisely gave many of his top military people extensive lands of their own. This generous act provided needed loyalty for William, and along with his own strength of character and iron will, allowed him to keep order during a time of tremendous upheaval throughout all of Europe.

The only significant reason to suggest that William the Conqueror plays any role whatsoever in the story just presented is this:

Hosta and Katti moved into their fine new house on a warm and mild day in the middle of an otherwise cold and miserable winter. They began a long and loving relationship for years to come.

The ancient Pueblo peoples of the southwestern United States did not have formal marriage ceremonies as we know them today. These two young people simply moved into their new home together where they took up life as husband and wife.

On the evening of their first night living together, Hosta presented Katti with a wonderfully smooth and snow-white cotton blanket. It was not perfectly made, and he looked forward to being able to produce better weavings in the future. But it was a gift from his heart and he told Katti the story of how he needed the skin of a spotted fawn to trade for enough cotton which he then used to make this gift of love and affection. Katti was very moved by the story and knew deep in her heart that this young man cared for her a great deal and would make a wonderful husband.

Hosta's father remained missing and never returned to the village. No one knows what became of him. Katti's father returned to Mesa Verde and lived out his life with his people.

Just before the fall harvest of this new year was over, Katti gave birth to a healthy son and she had no ill effects from the birth. Hosta's right leg recovered nicely throughout the year, although he noticed he could not run as fast as he used to. As he grew older this troublesome leg bothered him more and more, especially in the cold winter months. But the fracture had healed nicely and did not interfere much with living out his life.

The year in which all these quite common yet extraordinary events took place we identify today as the year 1066 A.D.

FURTHER *reading*

Much of the inspiration for the lives of the Archaic Pueblo Peoples came from a book entitled *Indians of the Mesa Verde,* written by Don Watson, and published by the Mesa Verde Museum Association located at the Mesa Verde National Park, near Cortez, Colorado.

If you would like to know more about the Anasazi people or archaeology of the Four Corners area, you might enjoy reading any one of these books:

THE ANASAZI, by J. Richard Ambler, Museum of Northern Arizona, Flagstaff, Arizona, 1989.

ANASAZI WORLD, by DeWitt Jones and Linda Cordell, Graphic Arts Center Publishing Company, Portland, Oregon, 1985.

ANCIENT TREASURER OF THE SOUTHWEST, by Franklin Folsom and Mary Elting Folsom, University of New Mexico Press, Santa Fe, New Mexico, 1994.

INDIANS OF THE AMERICAN SOUTHWEST, by Steven L. Walker, Camelback/Canyonlands Venture, Scottsdale, Arizona 1994.

THE ARCHAEOLOGY OF COLORADO, by E. Steve Cassells, Johnson Books, Boulder, Colorado, 1983.

DYNAMICS OF SOUTHWEST PREHISTORY, edited by Linda Cordell and George J. Gumerman, Smithsonian Institution Press, Washington, D.C., 1989.

EARTH WATER FIRE, by Norman T. Oppelt, Johnson Books, Boulder, Colorado, 1991.

MOTHER EARTH MERCANTILE, by Elizabeth M. Wheeler, Crow Canyon Archaeological Center, Cortez, Colorado, 1994.

ANCIENT NORTH AMERICA, by Brian M. Fagan, Thames and Hudson Publishing Company, New York, New York, 1995.

To receive more information about the many programs offered to the public, and for information on how you can participate in actual archaeological projects in the Four Corners area, contact The Crow Canyon Archaeological Center, 23390 County Road K, Cortez, Colorado 81321 (970) 565-8975.